# HOUSEWIVES' GUIDE
## TO ANTIQUES

# HOUSEWIVES' GUIDE TO ANTIQUES

### HOW TO GET THE MOST FOR YOUR MONEY WHEN FURNISHING YOUR HOME WITH ANTIQUES

*by*

## Leslie Gross

*Illustrated by the Author*

*An Exposition–Banner Book*

EXPOSITION PRESS         NEW YORK

EXPOSITION PRESS INC., 386 Park Avenue So., New York 16, N.Y.

FIRST EDITION

MANUFACTURED IN THE UNITED STATES OF AMERICA
BY GANIS & HARRIS, NEW YORK

To my husband

HARRY

# Preface

CAN YOU AFFORD a new Cadillac? If not, you will probably buy a Ford or a Chevy, or even one of those little foreign cars that are supposed to get so many miles to the gallon.

So it is with antiques.

The limited number of antiques with their hand-crafted manufacture has, along with that old bugaboo of supply and demand, created a high market value and sometimes even higher prices.

Way back in the days of individually made furniture there were "middle class" people with moderate incomes who managed nevertheless to furnish their homes in a comfortable, tasteful manner. They, like you, had a cultural awareness and an intellectual longing to be surrounded by lovely furnishings.

Here, then, is the purpose of this book: to aid you, of the Ford and Chevy pocketbook, in choosing antiques for your home. You need not be discouraged by the magnificent examples owned by museums or the very wealthy—there are good examples available within your price range.

Take heart, antique collector! There are wonderful buys awaiting you, once you learn where to look and what to look for.

L.G.

# Contents

# ILLUSTRATIONS

# Why Collect Antiques?

"A MAN'S HOME is his castle." There is no question but that this old adage is as true today as when it was first penned. Yes, a man's home *is* his castle, but it is his wife who must dust away the never-ending dust, who must clean and sweep, wash, wax and polish hundreds of hours every year to keep it that way.

A woman lives with her furniture so much more than her husband that her awareness of it surpasses his by a great deal. Husband and children live in the same house, true, but in a lesser number of hours and without the daily maintenance, so that as a consequence, they are not nearly so sensitive to, nor do they get the same enjoyment from, the furnishings.

## BEAUTY

In those long tedious hours of dusting and caring for her furniture, the housewife learns to know intimately each dust-collecting crevice, each carving and inlay, each adornment. An ugly piece of furniture soon turns a job, which at best can only be called dull, into one that makes her ready to scream.

Antiques have stood the test of time or they would not be antiques. Of course there were some poor examples made, just as there are today, but these were few. Many styles were of such excellence that they are still being made with little or no change in design. It is these lovely old pieces that the discriminating woman prefers to have in her home.

A poet once said, "A thing of beauty is a joy forever."

As long as you must have furniture anyway, you might as well have beautiful furniture. It costs no more, yet gives infinitely more pleasure.

Antique furniture encompasses so many styles and periods over a great many years, and in such a great variety, that there are enough varied examples to please every taste and budget.

## EASY UPKEEP

Having stood the ravages of time, antiques are not only still useful, but through the years of continued usage have attained a mellow beauty unmatched by modern copies. This is called "patina," which is the same term applied in the same way to your sterling silver. Do you remember that when you first purchased it, the salesman told you to use it often because it would become lovelier with age? At first you hesitated, then as the shiny newness began to mellow you knew he was right. Furniture, like fine silver, is to be used and enjoyed.

The small nicks and dents, the tiny scratches and worn parts add to the all-over beauty and are a vital part of the charm of antiques and are much desired. Many manufacturers of new furniture strive to gain this same effect, calling it a "distressed finish," which is often available at an additional cost.

These venerable signs of wear simplify upkeep too, for one more little mar caused by a careless guest need not mean expensive refinishing along with the annoyance of being without that needed table (and consequently having the lamp on the floor) several weeks while it is being fixed, as would be the case with new furniture.

In fact, many of the simpler country pieces made of durable pine and maple are practically child-proof.

## DURABILITY

In olden times furniture was individually built by hand in contrast to the fast assembly-line technique of today's methods. The best available woods were used along with sturdy construction.

Furniture was made to last. The very fact that they *are* antiques, and we still use them, proves that. Much of this same furniture will still be good long after their modern counterparts are serving as firewood.

## FOOL THE JONESES

Modern furniture, unlike the antique variety, is made in mass production and sold simultaneously in several stores within the same city, therefore its cost is easily known. Whether you try to keep up with the proverbial Joneses or not, is a personal matter, but in either case, with antique furnishings it is possible to have just as charming and lovely a home without divulging the family income.

There is no need to feel that the furniture is out of date after a few years and thus replace it at a strain against Husband's budget, when the furniture is still in good shape.

## BUY WHEN YOU WANT TO

Unlike modern suites of furniture, you can purchase individual pieces whenever you like. There are always other antiques which will blend with what you have already; and you can buy better items, one at a time as you wish (or as you can afford) rather than have to settle for lesser quality just because it is a set that has to be purchased all at once.

No matter which style you decide upon, there are always fine reproductions which you can use to fill in when the original is unavailable, or is too expensive.

## FUN

Specific antique items are not always found at the first store, and may require some enjoyable searching for just the exact article you desire. To "go antiquing" is as much a hobby as a way to furnish your home. Women are known for their love of shopping, and this is one way to get in a lot of shopping with a little buying.

## VERSATILITY

Antiques have the happy faculty of being very versatile. The same article can be at home in any of several different rooms. This makes it easy to change the appearance of the room by shifting different pieces of furniture to different rooms occasionally.

## THINK AHEAD

To the young couple just setting up housekeeping this versatility is a money-saving proposition. They can buy enough inexpensive antiques for their present needs to comfortably fill up their little apartment. With an eye to the future, and thought as to what additional requirements will be necessary, they can, as they can afford it, add finer furniture and relegate the first, less important, pieces to other rooms.

The simpler furniture first purchased can later be used to furnish a guest room, children's rooms and rumpus room. There is no wasteful buying of temporary furniture which will have to be discarded later. Just buy now what can be basically used anywhere, and make subsequent additions as you can.

## INVESTMENT—FACT OR FANCY?

There is considerable argument in some circles as to whether an antique is an "investment." Before you decide for yourself, let us find out what is meant by the word investment.

Cost is not the same thing as value, and should not be confused with it. Poor quality is no bargain at *any* cost.

Is it valuable just because it is old? Well, sometimes. Fragments dug up at Pompeii were painstakingly pieced together, the repaired items being valuable in that they were able to tell us about the lives and times of that ancient civilization. The museum curators esteem such articles highly, although they would not dream of putting them to their original uses. This is where the antique collector differs upon the question of value. You already know how your forebears lived. What you want in an antique is a fine old item that you can proudly display in your home, but more important, one that you can *use*, daily if necessary.

Age alone is no criterion of value. Unless you are the buyer for an historical society, an awkward, ungraceful monstrosity of furniture is of no value (except maybe as a curiosity) whether it was made one hundred or three hundred years ago, or if you have a friend who can get it for you wholesale straight from the manufacturer in Jamestown.

Don't buy something just because it is old! Age will not improve what was not good to start. Not all old wine is vintage champagne—sometimes it is just wine that has turned into vinegar. Antique furniture is no different.

Some antiques are more valuable than others of the same kind. Grace of design, fine workmanship, present condition, the amount of repair, if any—all these factors have an important bearing on the worth of any antique. Sturdiness is another important factor; a three-legged chair or a rickety table is hardly a wise buy. But besides this obvious example, there are numerous more subtle values to watch for. Two tables might be offered for the same price, and only close inspection will find small differences which would make one a better buy than the other. Therefore, the original cost of the antique must be in keeping with the value received.

If you have found a good, sturdy antique; one that is all original (meaning that it has had no repairs nor replacements) and is a good example of the style you want, is it a good investment?

The cost of this particular antique may be nearly the same, or slightly higher than (or in some cases, much higher than) that of a comparable piece bought new, all depending upon the individual antique and the part of the country in which you live.

However, with new furniture there will be a considerable loss when you sell it to buy another. With the antique, you are told, you will be able to profit by selling it in later years.

Economic conditions being as unstable as they are, this is not something upon which to count. Your antique may be of greater value in five years, or it may not. If you overpay now you will face a considerable loss in either event.

A good antique, though, is sure to bring you back a greater percentage of the original cost, even in bad times, than a similar item bought new.

The fact that antiques do not depreciate in value as does modern furniture means that your insurance on household goods will have to be kept up accordingly. Also in certain states, such as California, where the residents are taxed upon household goods, you will not have the benefit of the depreciation rate extended to you each year as with modern furniture.

## GRACIOUS LIVING

As to the gracious living to which the slick magazines so often refer, antiques are a splendid investment. As she dusts and cleans her house, any woman will feel happier when she has nice furnishings.

A lovely home is something that offers enjoyment in many ways: comfort for the body, beauty for the eye, and contentment for the mind in knowing that, "Be it ever so humble . . ." *your* home is the nicest place in the world.

# What Is an Antique?

## ANTIQUES DEFINED

WHEN DOES AN ITEM stop being just "old" and become eligible for the veneration of being called "antique"? In 1930 Congress passed a law stating that antiques are items made prior to the year 1830. This is the legal definition, which is used chiefly for import duties and taxes.

Today there is a general agreement among dealers and collectors alike that anything made one hundred or more years ago is entitled to be called an antique. This is the age usually referred to in speaking of antique furniture, and the most commonly used meaning of the word.

However, due to the sentimental value of many items belonging to elderly or deceased members of their families, and the mistaken idea of the true ages of these treasures, (Why, it must have been in Grandma's attic forever!) some people refer to anything old or obsolete as being "antique." This is a common misnomer among the well-meaning but misinformed. There is not much you can do when someone shows you a late Victorian chair which was owned by her Aunt Agatha, and proudly tells you that it is two hundred years old, except try to smile and mutter something noncommittal like, "My, how interesting."

This book will include such "antiques" from Grandma's attic because: they are thought of as antiques, they are plentiful in quantity, and they still have lots of use left in them.

## OLD AND RICKETY

Does friend Husband shudder at the mention of antique furniture? It may well be that he has come into contact with poor specimens and has been told that, "It's rickety because it's so old—it's an antique, you know."

This time Husband is right. If a chair is too wobbly to be used, it should be either discarded, or, if it is of excellent style and workmanship but suffers from years of misuse and abuse, it should be placed in a museum where it can be seen but not used.

To be of any value, an antique must be sturdy and in good enough condition so that the man of the house can heap his 180 pounds in comfort, and the guests can sit where they please without warnings of the imminent danger of collapse.

A good piece of antique furniture was well made and if it received common-sense wear and tear it should be as strong today as when it was new.


## FAKES

Don't let yourself be taken in by the interesting stories about the "little old lady who owned this originally." Sellers of antique furniture and used-car dealers are noted for this approach. These fables are heard so often that it leads one to believe that two generations ago the world was populated by sweet little old ladies who did nothing but buy old furniture from sweeter, older ladies. As with the beds slept in by George Washington, or the furniture brought over on the *Mayflower,* these stories, even when repeated in full belief of their authenticity, must be taken with a grain of salt. If you were to believe that all the furniture was as claimed, you also have to believe that the *Mayflower* was twice the size of the liner *Queen Mary,* and stowed to the gunnels; and that the father of our country was a traveling salesman.

Your own good sense will lead you to examine the furniture carefully before purchasing, thereby sparing yourself expensive mistakes. There will be times when, on the other hand, you will be able to discover a good antique hiding under a dull coat of paint or masquerading as "just that old chest down in the cellar."

Lumber was abundant in the olden days, and so you will find that large boards were commonly used. Table tops as well as chest tops and sides, especially those of pine, maple and cherry, were often made out of a single wide board which might measure from 18 to 30 inches wide with very few tiny knots, if any. This lumber was cut in odd sizes to utilize as much of the tree as was possible. In contrast, today's furniture is made of many small boards skillfully glued and stained. If you look closely at the new furniture you can see this by the difference in grain of the different individual boards. (From the top) veneer will give the appearance of one board, but underneath you will be able to detect a different wood grain.

Another fact to remember about authentic antiques is that along with being of odd, unstandardized sizes, the lumber was dressed by hand so that the planing was not smooth as is the case with modern tools. If you run your fingers very lightly across an old board you can feel the difference between hand-dressed lumber and the modern machine-processed kind; this is even more apparent on the undersides and the insides of old furniture.

Marks of tools from the old slow lathes and straight saw kerfs differ from modern equipment which leaves circular saw marks and perfectly smooth turnings from modern lathes capable of as many as 3,500 r.p.m.

Not all furniture was constructed with dovetails, but when found, they are larger and irregular and the "patina" (that soft color and the minute marks, dents, and scratches found on old furniture) will be upon the sawed ends and will be even in color all over the article. This is difficult to duplicate and one reason why antiques with extensive repairs are sanded is to disguise the newly added portions.

Wooden pegs were often used in place of nails. This was done because it provided better construction, not because of the scarcity of nails. These pegs were whittled by hand and are never perfectly round. They project slightly higher than the flat surfaces.

Hand-forged nails are to be found in furniture made before 1790, and usually have square heads. Hand-forged nails were made up until about 1870. Although crude machine nails appeared around 1790, they were produced in small quantities. Screws were made entirely by hand as early as 1588 and continued in usage until crude machine-made screws appeared about 1810-45; all of these were blunt on the end and had to be started with a gimlet. After 1850 sharp, pointed modern screws came into use. Handmade items were never as true, never as round and perfect as those the machine turned out. Some were well made, but close inspection will show the difference. The joiners and cabinetmakers never countersank nails and puttied the resulting indentations, as is the practice today, so if you see furniture with this characteristic, you can be sure it is either of late vintage or that it has been extensively repaired.

Mouldings are another determining factor of age in furniture. Early moulding was large and simple and a trifle uneven. Before 1840 they were usually held in place by brads or pegs rather than glue.

All wood shrinks in the course of time due to atmospheric changes. In antiques this is evident on round boards and turned parts, such as legs, because the wood shrinkage takes place across the grain in the width, but not in length, thus making the round parts a trifle ovoid in shape. This is not always readily apparent to the eye, but can be detected by the use of a pair of calipers.

The wear on chair legs and rungs will be uneven, and even the best furniture will have some visible marks from normal usage and wear on some portions, especially the bottom few inches where mops, brooms, and, later, vacuum cleaners have bumped during the years. These characteristics can be created with the use of a wood rasp and other tools by an unscrupulous person with the intent to defraud.

Signs of wear and tear will vary with the individual article. Some have many, others hardly any at all, according to how well they were cared for. Their venerable battle scars are honorable and should *not* be removed. Of course, a broken leg or missing handle must be repaired or replaced to be made serviceable but it should be kept in mind that *any repair depreciates value.*

There are many ingenious ways these venerable signs of age can be produced spuriously, and the amateur is advised to study further and to seek professional opinions before investing any sizeable amount of money in a single antique. For average purchases, however, these signs will be sufficient to protect you against most common frauds.

## GETTING STUCK

Every collector gets "stuck" with a spurious antique at one time or another. Even the most expert will on occasion be fooled by a clever fraud. This is as much a part of collecting antiques as when the housewife finds a bad melon upon cutting into what appeared so perfect at the market.

Careless or incomplete examination of the antique is the usual cause of this mishap. The author, who should know better, did the same thing a few years ago by purchasing a small chest of drawers which seemed to be in excellent shape except for a slight crack across the top board and several coats of dark paint. Upon removing the paint, it was found that the "small crack" was in reality the junction of two boards, and that the thick paint concealed wood of three different species. The only way to salvage the money spent was to repaint the chest, which was done with a soft green decorated in white; this gave a far different appearance than desired.

Since no one likes to admit that he has been fooled, I quickly change the subject when this chest is noticed and tell about the real bargain I stumbled upon in obtaining a small pine primitive chest with handles of black walnut as deep and rich in color as bitter-sweet chocolate. The locks, I discovered after the purchase, are handmade and in perfect working order.

Human nature being what it is, you will hear many such tales of fabulous buys, yet few of the mistakes we all make.

So take heart, new collector! Mistakes will happen to the best of us, but you can avoid many pitfalls by knowing what to look for, and then by carefully scrutinizing before buying. You cannot carry a string of implements, like an over-grown charm bracelet consisting of calipers, steel straight edge, magnifying glass, tape measure, and flashlight; but you can run your fingers over the back to feel for hand-planing, you can take out the drawers, examine the insides, turn small furniture upside down, and otherwise inspect it carefully in all respects. The more money involved, the more inspection necessary. No reputable dealer will object—on the contrary, he will respect you for your knowledge.

## ENLIST HUSBAND'S HELP

This is a good time to get your Husband interested in antiques. He already knows something about woodworking and construction methods, and is familiar with such terms as dovetails, mortise and tenon, lathe, turning, jigsaw, jack plane, and so forth. Possibly he enjoys puttering around in his basement workshop.

Once he learns what to look for and how to determine genuine antiques, he will take a greater interest and be willing to shop with you rather than just yawn and tell you to, "Buy whatever you like, dear, but don't spend too much."

Two heads are always better than one; while he becomes an "expert" on detecting fakes, you can bone up on styles and periods. Shop and buy together—it is more fun with four informed, alert eyes instead of just your own two, and there is much less chance of being stuck with a fake. Knowing the difference, your Husband may well surprise you by urging you to spend just a little more than you had hoped for, because of a better value than what you would have bought alone fearing his disapproval. After all, even though we women are considered shrewder shoppers, he did earn the money and he wants the most for each dollar.

## GLORIFYING

Many antiques were made quite plain. An unscrupulous cabinet-maker may add carving or inlay, or may take a heavy Empire style bedpost and re-turn or recarve it to resemble a more delicate style of another period. This is referred to as "glorifying" the furniture, and is done in order to make the furniture appear older than it is or more ornate and thus increase its value. For the same reason, parts of broken furniture may be saved and rebuilt into other or smaller pieces. Some of these "late marriages" may contain parts which are, in themselves, quite original. For instance, a table top might be salvaged, and the skirt and legs from another added; or a smaller table might be made from a larger one which is badly damaged.

Some furniture is converted into other more in demand on the current market. Plain cupboards are cut into welsh dressers; flat-top highboys have been known to be divided and used separately as lowboy and chest after legs had been added to the top section; rockers can be added to plain chairs, and so on.

Knowledge of styles and construction, along with careful inspection, is your protection against these glorifications as well as against spurious antiques.

## REPRODUCTIONS

Just because you cannot afford to buy certain valuable antiques is no sound reason to deny yourself the pleasure of seeing the same exquisite forms in your home.

Copies of good furniture have been made ever since the styles were first introduced. Some of these same copies were made in the same manner as the originals although at a later date than the actual period, and are now well over a hundred years old themselves. These are not, in the general meaning of the word, reproductions, for that term denotes modern furniture made in the same styles.

In many circles, reproductions are wrongly looked down upon, for they do serve a useful purpose. Antiques are not as readily obtainable as new furniture, and there are times when you might need another chair or small table for that certain blank spot in the front hall, and not be able to find just what you want in the antique shops. Then again, since antiques were made in limited quantities, there are certain examples which are highly desirable and yet so scarce as to make the price prohibitive when they are available.

So you cannot afford to go to Paris and buy an original Dior dress. That does not mean that you cannot be well dressed; you can still go to one of the better department stores in your town and buy a copy which will be just as becoming to you. In the right color and with the correct accessories you can look just as smart (in a healthy American way) as the skinniest Parisian model. You do not feel ashamed of the copy, nor try to pretend it is an original; it becomes you, you enjoy it. There is no difference with furniture. You buy the best you can afford, arrange it comfortably, add colors which become you, your choice of accessories, and—*voilà!* You enjoy it.

Some upholstered sofas and chairs, such as Queen Anne and Chippendale, have only the legs (and possibly stretchers) showing, while the rest of the framework is hidden from view. Most of these will require new upholstery to recover that which is badly worn, or to better suit the color scheme of your individual home. Would it not then, be wiser to order a new wing chair in the exact style you want and to put the difference in money you save towards a fine desk or chest of drawers, where you can see and enjoy the construction and mellow old wood that you are paying for? If your money is unlimited, of course you will want to buy only the best originals.

There are times when a good reproduction can be an asset to your home. Let me stress the word "good." Some furniture manufacturers make faithful copies of antiques, true to line and style, but with modern methods. Some of these are finished with the previously mentioned "distressed finish" which duplicates the tiny dents and mars of time, not to deceive the buyer, but in order to soften the newness and that just-off-the-assembly-line appearance. These will harmonize nicely with your genuine antiques and serve to beautify your home where the originals are not available. Other manufacturers toss together some woods in the semblance of furniture and call it a reproduction, even though it has been debased until it is an eyesore.

By studying the original antiques through your library and museum, you will learn to identify the desired features of the originals and thus know what to seek in reproductions. Select only those good of design, faithful to style, and sound of construction.

# Antiques Versus Modern Living

## INCONGRUOUSNESS

THERE IS NOTHING INCONGRUOUS about combining antiques with the most modern surroundings. We human beings are complex organisms that can enjoy all sorts of divergent notions at the same time. The man who roundly curses out his business competitor, shouting, "They can't do that to me," is the same man who will think nothing of drying the dinner dishes; the gentlewoman of the past is no more, today it is the same woman who dons faded blue jeans to scrub the kitchen floor in the morning who will emerge in the afternoon, bathed, polished, and fashionably dressed at the P.T.A. meeting, looking for all the world as if she had done nothing but primp all day. The timid white-haired lady you see sitting in the park on a spring day crocheting daintily, is the same woman who attends the wrestling matches every Friday night and screams for blood; the girl roller-derby champ listens to symphonic music on her hi-fi set for relaxation.

With such apparently contradicting interests in other fields of daily living, it is not strange to find any type of antique collected by the most unlikely people.

Collect what you will enjoy. Use your antiques. Display them attractively. If you like anything enough to spend time and money collecting it, then it *belongs;* it is as much a part of you as the way you wear your hair, and will fit into your home beautifully.

## BEST OF THE PAST

It is unnecessary to duplicate antique living with exact replicas of the rooms as furnished years ago. You do not use oil for your lighting, nor rely on open fireplaces for heat, so there is no reason to feel bound to furnish your home exactly as our forebears did just because you appreciate their fine furniture that has been handed down as antiques.

By taking the spirit of the days gone by, along with the furniture, it is possible to adapt antiques to modern living and have the best of the past along with all the comforts and conveniences of today. Thomas Jefferson, with his constant improvements and modernizations in his home at Monticello, would have been the first to agree that the fine furniture and interesting accessories culled from the long ago can be completely compatible with the miracles of modern living.

Gracious living, as the magazines write about it, refers to no special era nor period. Comfort, pleasant surroundings, and livability are always in fashion.

## MODERN ARCHITECTURE

You need not have an old house to provide authentic background for your antiques. The Cape Cod house with its familiar block shape and symmetrical roof is a common sight even today; its simple design has endured in the middle- and lower-cost housing field because it is comparatively easy and economical to build. Shingled or clapboarded, white or any color of the rainbow, it is still popular with contractor and owner alike.

Even sprawling ranch houses need not be a barrier to collecting and using antique furniture. Lovely old furniture will give substantial character to an otherwise unexciting house.

## INDIVIDUALITY

Buying a house is in many ways the same as buying a pound of hamburger. A woman buys both for the same reasons: because her family likes it, because it is the best buy for the money, and because there is so much she can do with it. There are so many ways to suit your family's taste, from substantial meatloaf, through ever-popu-

lar broiled hamburger patties. It can be extended with bread, oat-
meal or rice. It can become fancy Swedish meatballs or spicy
Italian meat sauce, or whatever else you like best. So it is with a
house.

Antiques allow for a greater range of individuality even in
tract houses. A builder erects a row of tract houses which are all
alike except for the color and the numbers on the door. The houses
will remain alike until they are sold and the new owners move in,
then they begin to show changes. Drive down a street of tract
houses that are five or ten years old and you will notice how different they look from the new rubber stamp appearance they first had.

Your home is an extension of your personality. Every woman
should have the opportunity to express herself and to see to the
comfort of her family in her own way. This is what changes a house
into a home.

The use of antiques in decorating that dream home allows for
the greater expression of individuality because there is a larger
area from which to draw—all the past.

Like attending a party to discover another woman wearing the
same dress, finding the exact suite of modern furniture in her
neighbor's identical tract house, can embarrass a woman.

A particular antique might be found in another's home, but
certainly not a duplication of your whole room of antique furniture. The selection of individual pieces and the groupings and arrangements are all your own.

## ADDITIONAL CLOSET SPACE

Modern or old-fashioned, your house can benefit by additional
storage space.

Start with a convenient commode in the front foyer. It will
provide a much-needed hiding place for rubbers, galoshes, umbrella, plastic boots, rock salt for chasing snow, and that small
doormat reserved for rainy weather. It can also hold a boot jack;
this handy item is just the thing for removing those stubborn
galoshes or snow boots without having to bend over and struggle

with them, or it can help you out of rubbers without getting your hands all muddy. Your guests also will appreciate your boot jack when they visit you during inclement weather.

Placed near the back door, a pine dry sink, although not a particularly beautiful piece of furniture, will be an excellent receptacle for gardening gloves, the old shoes or rubbers you wear to water the lawn, pruning shears, your favorite trowel, packages of seeds, extra plant stakes, and even the dog's ball—the one that you won't let him have indoors for fear he will leave it where someone will trip over it. The sink part of the dry sink has seen lots of water in its time, so you need not hesitate to utilize it as a good place for sorting and arranging your flowers as you bring them into the house. This is also a good place to drop that heavy bag of groceries while you take off your coat.

For that basement recreation room a marble-top commode, possibly painted a gay color, can become a bar. The marble top is alcohol resistant and the bottom hides your liquor along with the cocktail glasses between parties.


## OUTDOOR LIVING

Do you have a large patio or just a postage stamp sized porch? A large elaborate barbecue pit or just a tiny folding grill? In any case you want to get the most of those hot, lazy summer evenings.

Old kerosene lamps can be found in several sizes and many pleasing designs—some so simple of design that they look positively modern. Use them just as they are for outdoor lighting. Let Husband take care of the lamps and the kerosene just as he does the gasoline for his power mower.

The long-handled cooking tools that once provided protection from open fireplace cooking are ideal for your barbecue.

Use woodenware as much as possible to save worry about breaking good dishes or bowls. Do not hesitate to wash woodenware articles! Scrub them well, but avoid soaking in water. It is better to have a slightly warped bowl, knowing it is clean enough to eat from, than an unwarped one which has you in doubt.

Some women wash and sterilize old chamber pots to use as

expendible punch bowls for outdoor parties. They can also be used for soup tureens, and in either case will be a sure "conversation piece."

Large copper and brass kettles will make attractive planters for your lawn or patio and need not even be leakproof. A few holes on the bottom will provide drainage as well as a reasonable price for you; with colorful petunias spilling over the top no one will ever know.

Weather vanes and door knockers can be found in many shapes and add to the appearance of any house.

## GARDEN FURNITURE

You can use furniture which was made especially for the garden, such as the formal, cast iron variety, or you can humorously make use of whatever is not fine enough for the inside of your house. A coat of exterior enamel paint in white or any color which harmonizes with your house will transform even the roughest cast-off into an acceptable garden seat. Here the quality will not be the first consideration, but price. Look for poorer specimens to be used this way, as they will be exposed to the elements all summer you will not want to misuse a fine antique this way.

Old wagon seats with legs added to bring them up to a comfortable height, and gaily painted, are most attractive. A discarded cobbler's bench will provide both table area and a seat. Split log benches are a rustic delight.

A place to sit makes your garden much more enjoyable. Let your imagination run wild; use whatever catches your fancy. If you feel artistic you might try gay peasant designs and motifs.

## SENTIMENTALITY

So often there are treasured items handed down from Grandmother to mother to daughter. These have great sentimental value regardless of their intrinsic worth and should not be relegated to the attic. They can be used or displayed where they will be seen and enjoyed every day.

A pleasing background will enhance the beauty of these relics, and they can be harmonious with even the most modern house. This blending of the present with the past is nostalgically compatible with any decor and any architecture.

# Antiques for Every Taste

THERE ARE AS MANY KINDS of antiques as there were people who made and used them. This allows that there will be antique furniture to suit your needs no matter what your personal tastes.

The essence of a house is that it must express the family it houses. Your home is actually an extension of yourself and your family: of your requirements, your work and play habits, and your individual and collective preferences. All these variables must be taken into consideration when furnishing a home.

## SIZE OF FAMILY

The size of your family will effect the kind of antiques you will buy for your home. A family consisting of just a husband and wife will be able to utilize the finest in their home. Add some small children and the requirements demand more rugged furnishings. Older children are not so destructive, yet they need more space to stretch and a chance to express their parts as members of the family unit. Any members of the older generation living with you will also have their requirements as to privacy and conveniences which may at times conflict with others.

Knowing your family as only you can, keep all those requirements in mind when selecting antiques in the neighborhood "Shoppee."

Do not let yourself be swept away by a spur of the moment purchase which will be impractical in your home.

## VARIETY

The great variety of styles allows for an equal variety of choice: the woman who feels most comfortable in chic tailored clothes, shirtmaker dresses, plain shirts and skirts, might very well choose the straight lines of Sheraton styling as her preference; while at the same time her sister who prefers lacy garments, ribbons, jabots and bouffant skirts would rather have frilly Victorian furniture in her home.

Fussy Victorian, delicate Hepplewhite, graceful Queen Anne, heavy, sturdy Empire, bold, masculine Chippendale, tailored, straight-lined Sheraton, casual country pines: different characteristics to appeal to different personalities—yet each has its honored place in the hearts of antique lovers. Some styles appeal more to certain people than others, and some people have more than one favorite.

Whatever your tastes, there is just the antique for you, all you have to do is search for it—and that's half the fun.

## HUSBAND CAN HELP

Encourage friend Husband to help select your furniture. He has to live there too, and who knows? He may just come up with a suggestion that will add a spark to an otherwise plain room.

Shopping around from store to store, diligently seeking out that one special piece of furniture you need is not always to a man's liking. If, on the other hand, you do the preliminary shopping to eliminate what is *not* suitable, then Husband will not object so strenuously to looking in just one or two shops to help make the final decision. Just as a mother avoids asking, "Would you like some green beans for dinner?" by the subtle question, "Which do you prefer, green beans or peas?" thus keeping the child too busy deciding which of two alternatives to choose to realize that he did not really want either; so it often is with the shrewd antique shopper. Let your Husband decide which of two or three specific antiques he would prefer to have in your home.

## ENTERTAINMENT REQUIREMENTS

The amount and kind of entertaining that you do will have some bearing upon the antique furnishings for your home. Formal entertainment of your Husband's business associates, important social obligations and stuffy business contacts require a more formal decor than entertaining of a casual nature, consisting mostly of family and personal friends.

A bridge party for the "girls," a cocktail party, a summer barbecue, Junior's Boy Scout troop meeting—each so different from all the others, and yet the same house must provide, and provide graciously, for each event.

## DIFFERENT STYLES

It is not always possible to furnish a house completely in one style, nor is it a sound idea to do so. Individuality is as desirable as privacy in any home. With so many varied activities taking place under the same roof and often including different people, it is an only natural outcome that there should be a change of styles from room to room.

A "family room" or "game room" done in casual country pine is ideal for suburban moderns. Lately there has been a trend for this separation, this room apart from the living room, positioned near the kitchen or in the basement. This allows the living room proper to be used for entertaining and for "dress up" occasions much like the old-fashioned parlor, rather than for the daily play and T.V. area. With your pine and maple furniture taking the daily wear and tear, you can then put your finer carved mahogany in the less used living room. If, however, you have only one room for both purposes, then you have the choice of using either casual or formal or a median between the two, depending upon whether your family consists of all adults or adults and small children.

For other rooms you might choose entirely different styles.

## MIXING STYLES

Different periods and styles for different rooms make an interesting house. When several people live in the same house, the change from one room to the next can allow for individuality as well as to provide for different activities. Dainty furnishings for baby sister; bolder, rugged furniture for brother; nostalgic for Grandpa if he lives with you: subtle little changes in personality from the body of the house.

A lot of thought must go into the mixing of different styles in order to have a pleasant blending of one to another. Careless mixing will only result in a hopeless hodge-podge confusing to the eye and the intellect.

In choosing antiques for your home pay heed to the similarities of styles. Periods which followed each other generally overlapped styles, often resulting in the making of more than one style simultaneously. The style changes were never abrupt. Duncan Phyfe, the cabinetmaker, was turning out Sheraton furniture along with his Directoire and early Empire. There are chairs which show characteristics of both Queen Anne and Chippendale, which generally are referred to as Georgian, after the King Georges' ruling subsequent to Queen Anne. Hepplewhite and Sheraton used the same designs and details many times, resulting in confusion on both sides of the Atlantic Ocean, since it is difficult to tell one from the other in certain pieces of furniture. Later Sheraton styles melted into Directoire, which in turn flowed uninterruptedly into Empire. In fact, so close are the styles that in many circles Directoire is not differentiated at all, that furniture just being called early Empire. Late Empire is close to early Victorian in many instances.

The transition from one style to another occasionally produced furniture examples which defy classification and can properly be used anywhere they look good.

## ANTIQUES WITH MODERN

In combining antiques with modern furniture—if you must—try to use restraint. Extremes of each kind will not look good together, so if you must have some modern pieces use those with similar lines. That is, avoid having a straight-lined, square, angular article next to a curvacious, heavily carved one; or a small one dwarfed by a huge neighbor. Choose woods of the same kind or finish.

Similarity will help overcome differences.

## WHAT ABOUT TELEVISION?

Television cabinets and radios are made in limited styles and there is not much you can do about it. Since they represent an important aspect in today's hurried existence, we may as well go along with the inevitable. It was a wise man who first coined the phrase, "If you can't beat 'em, join 'em."

Take a comfortable arrangement of your furniture including the T.V. set, a pleasant color scheme, good antiques, and interesting accessories, mix well, and no one will think twice about the television set in the midst of antiques.

Table models and portables give a greater choice of arrangements than the larger console types. Recently several manufacturers have put excellent smaller sets on the market, some with colored cases that can be inconspicuous against a painted wall of the same color.

One woman solved the T.V. problem by using a curly maple drop-leaf table holding a 17-inch portable in the same color as part of the wallpaper design in the room. The expanse of table which shows around the television set helps create a pleasing transition from screen to antiques.

## WOODS

Certain woods have an affinity for each other and can therefore be used together with great harmony.

Mahogany and cherry, both being slightly reddish, look good together. Pine, maple, birch and other lighter colored woods may be used interchangeably. Maple and cherry are often found in the same article. Old pine has a soft color which blends well with walnut. Curly maple, bird's-eye maple and tiger-striped maple are of a fancy nature and go well with plain maple, with more elaborate, and with simpler furniture. Bird's-eye is generally found as a veneer rather than solid wood like other members of the curly maple family. Walnut can be used with mahogany, unless the latter has a very dark, or a very red finish.

## COLOR

The least costly, and the most often overlooked element in interior decoration is color. This simple expedient can change your room to an almost unbelievable degree.

Have no fear of color. Use it boldly as you choose. You certainly would not buy a dress if the salesgirl told you, "It doesn't look *bad*." Then why buy a rug or a sofa in some wishy-washy color on the advice of a clerk who has nothing more favorable to say than, "It's neutral and won't clash with anything else." Neutrality is something for politicians to debate; not a condition for the house you have to live in every day.

Use your favorite colors for your home. Surround yourself with the colors you like best.

There are certain colors and groups of colors associated with the different periods when they were fashionable along with the styles of furniture which prevailed at those same times. At times strong color, at other times pastel tints were the favorite color schemes. These have been noted with the styles accompanying them in Chapter 6.

The colors concurrently popular with specific antiques can be a starting point for your particular home's interior decoration; although you can properly use any colors you prefer.

The color scheme chosen for your home must concern other factors besides just the furniture. First in importance, is to be surrounded by colors which you and your family find pleasing. Choose those colors which are your favorites and those that are the most becoming to you.


## YOU

In the final analysis, your home is you! Don't be hidebound by any rule books. Read the rules, and then rely upon your own good taste. Please yourself and your family; you are the ones that live there. When your home is just the way you find it most attractive, your visitors will enjoy it too.

# Availability of Antiques

## MUSEUMS

MANY FINE EXAMPLES of antique furniture have found their way into our museums. These, then, since they belong to the museums, in a way become everybody's property. Being on display for all to see, these excellent pieces benefit the whole populace and are doubly valuable in this respect.

It is important that there be displays set up in the various historical societies so that this important phase of the past will be permanently preserved.

This is fine as far as it goes, but there is another side of this subject which is less beneficent. Consider the individual who spends a pleasant afternoon at the local museum or historical society viewing some superb examples of the carver's and cabinet-maker's art, then goes out in futile quest of similar items for her own domicile. This is particularly apt to occur in the larger cities, such as New York—where Philadelphia highboys shake hands with Rhode Island block front furniture in the famed Metropolitan Museum.

## HEIRLOOMS

The most highly desirable articles were made in limited quantities; some now reside in the better museums and some are heirlooms in the mansions of the wealthy. They are proudly handed down from one generation of blue bloods to the next, with no thought of selling.

## PRICES

From time to time venerable items will be put on the open market, where they often carry price tags that stagger the imagination. The better specimens are, all too often, priced way beyond the purse of the average collector.

These impressive and meritorious articles are now, as they were when first made, for the wealthy. But do not despair! There were many people one hundred years or more ago who were educated to, and intellectually aware of, the artistic merit of fine furnishings; yet who were in modest financial circumstances, even as you and I. These people were able to furnish their homes in excellent fashion.

Even when simplicity was substituted for the elegance of the higher-priced articles, it was without loss of beauty or of craftsmanship, for these antiques are every bit as lovely as the more elaborate ones.

The difference sometimes was in the wood used. Instead of the expensive imported mahogany, local cabinetmakers used native woods. Some connoisseurs prefer mahogany, yet there is a latent spark of patriotism in all of us which points out, truthfully, that our Yankee know-how was able to produce articles just as fine, and in some instances (such as block fronts and Philadelphia-style highboys) even superior to anything imported. This is why many actually prefer their furniture to be all American, even down to the use of native woods.

Fancy grained woods were often chosen for furniture which had no carving, in order to give the finished product a more elegant appearance. By eliminating the carving, many man-hours, and thus much expense, was saved. Where carving appears, there are varying degrees of elaborateness, the simpler being just as old and equally appropriate for your home.

Fine lacquered furniture with the original finish in good condition will be high in price; but the simpler painted items will be proportionately less, and therefore good examples will be found within your price range.

Available antique furniture ranges from the elaborately carved and inlaid to the completely unadorned; from the finest imported woods to abundant domestic products; from artistically lacquered highboys in the Chinese fashion to primitive Pennsylvania Dutch dower chests; from Sheraton fancy chairs to mass-produced Hitchcock-type chairs.

An excess of surface decoration is no criterion for fine furniture. There is no need to gild the lily.

Pleasing proportions, beauty of line and shape, good construction and condition, patina, appropriate hardware, and very little restoration, if any—all these help to make an antique desirable, and all can be found in simple as well as elaborately decorated furniture.

Good taste should not be confused with elaborateness; they can, and do exist separately.

With these things in mind you can "go antiquing" with the assurance that you will be able to find fine antiques for your home despite financial limitations.

## AVAILABILITY

The bulk of the antiques within the lower-price range will be found mainly in Empire and Victorian styles.

Country pine furniture is also abundant, although considerable "picking over" must be done in order to find the better examples. The so-called "Primitive" or "Provincial" furniture falls into this broad classification. By selective choosing you can find many delightful examples. Since so much country furniture was made by hand in the olden ways long after mechanized production took over more sophisticated manufacturers, there is a great deal of this charmingly primitive furniture still around. Completely in accord with the casual living in modern suburban areas, this furniture is as popular today as when it was first made.

Fancy chairs were made as early as 1790 and continued in popularity over a long period of time. There were about fifty manufacturers producing fancy, painted chairs during 1810 to 1860, including the famous Lambert Hitchcock. Many reproductions have been made of these and the prospective buyer is again urged to carefully inspect before purchasing.

The always fashionable Windsor chair has been made constantly from 1725, suggesting that there still should be quite a few around.

Therefore, considering the vast amount of furniture made, there is sure to be a large quantity available for today's homemakers. By discriminating selection you will find many lovely items to grace your home. Astute shopping will enable you to furnish your home attractively without having to resort to bank robbery.

# Styles and Periods

## AMERICAN FURNITURE

THE FIRST AMERICAN FURNITURE was made by the Colonists not long after their arrival in Virginia in 1607. This very early furniture was limited in scope, consisting mainly of tables, chests, chests of drawers, stools and a few chairs.

The furniture they made for their homes in the new world was the same kind they had known back in England. This tie between the American Colonies and England remained very strong all during our Colonial days prior to Independence in 1776. This influence is demonstrated by the early cabinetmakers who often copied English designs directly, occasionally adapting them to suit American tastes. Some innovations were entirely of American design; the finest of these being the magnificent block front furniture from Rhode Island.

The furniture described in this book is American and the mention of foreign furniture will be dealt with only where it seriously influenced the native product.

## DATES

Because communication methods were unbelievably slow compared with today's instantaneous ones, the styles which originated in England were fashionable here at a date considerably later.

In the same way the rural districts lagged behind the larger cities. The country cabinetmakers did not follow styles as closely as those in the cities and often continued the use of a style years after it had passed out of fashion in the cities.

Some styles were made continuously over a long period of years because of their popularity.

All this makes dating of furniture an approximate, rather than an exact, science. For instance, a particular item cannot with any certainly be pinpointed at 1727; but it can be accurately dated as "circa 1730" (circa means about). These dates are more than adequately accurate.

## COLONIAL

"Colonial" is a name given to the furniture made while our country was one of the English colonies and covers the years from 1620 to 1776 or a little later.

There is no definite Colonial style as such. What is considered Colonial is actually the typically American version of the furniture popular during that time.

Simpler, plainer furniture was better suited to the needs of the settlers than the finer, more elaborate furniture being made at the same time in England. The wealthier people in the big cities followed English styles more closely than other segments of the population.

Native woods such as pine, ash, hickory, apple, pear, cherry and maple were used, and reed and rush seats were common. Slatback chairs, Carver chairs, settles, hutch tables, gateleg tables, Welsh cupboards, pierced tin pie cupboards, board chests, blanket chests, butterfly tables—all sorts of the simpler furniture can be classified under this heading.

## FEDERAL

The term "Federal" refers to the years following the Revolutionary War against England when our young Federation of the thirteen states won Independence. This period is generally considered from 1776 to 1830.

There was a turning away from things English then, so during this time French influence was felt through Empire styles. American cabinetmakers adapted the currently fashionable French Empire into a more suitable version: American Empire.

The bald eagle, a symbolic emblem of our new nation, gained

immense popularity and was used frequently. Stars often appeared, generally in the number of thirteen. Red, white and blue became a familiar color combination.

## JACOBEAN

Jacobean is the term used to cover all English style furniture from the reign of James I to James II—1603 to 1688.

The first furniture made on our side of the ocean, then, was the same Jacobean that was being used in England at that time.

What little furniture was produced during this time was sturdy, but stiff and uncomfortable. It consisted mainly of chests which were paneled and carved, cupboards, trestle tables and wainscot chairs. Also the Brewster and Carver chairs were made with numerous spindles filling their straight frames. They take their names from two distinguished Colonists.

Flemish scrolls, paneling, applied split spindles and carving, along with rush seats, Spanish feet, bulbous ornaments and twist or spiral carvings were the decorative features, making this straight massive furniture formal as well as formidable in appearance.

Oak was the most popular wood used along with some of the abundant pine. Oak paneling with linenfold and Tudor rose carving completed what must have been dreary interiors.

## WILLIAM AND MARY

It was during the time from 1688 to 1702 that furniture began to develop along slender, more graceful lines and become more adapted to comfort. William and Mary brought back with them to England Dutch preferences as well as the men to produce these styles.

Entirely different than the straight uncompromising furniture it succeeded, this style began the trend toward the attractive furniture which was to follow.

Bun feet, Spanish scroll feet, and serpentine stretchers appeared, along with the characteristic legs with their inverted cup turnings. Dutch cabriole legs were introduced and became much

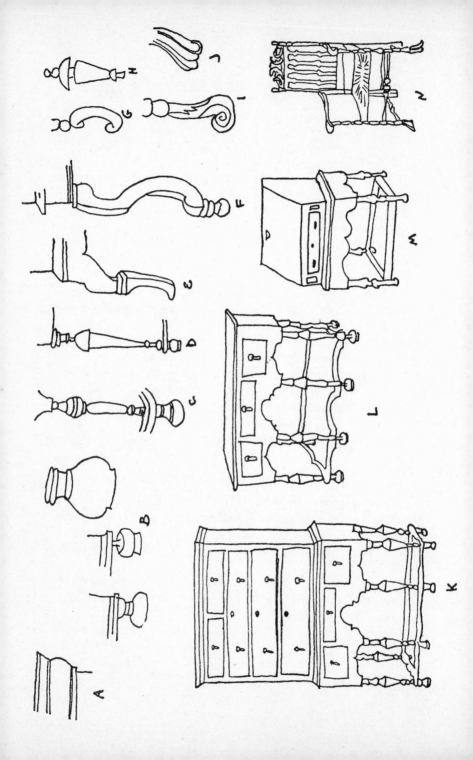

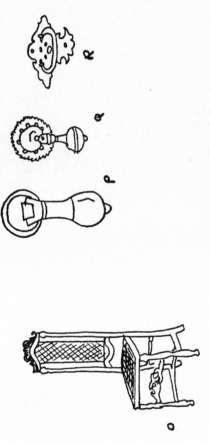

# WILLIAM AND MARY

*A* cornice (top molding), *B* bun feet, *C, D, E, F, G* legs (*E* Dutch cabriole leg, *D* trumpet leg), *H* trumpet foot, *I* scroll foot, *J* Spanish foot, *K* highboy, *L* lowboy, *M* desk on frame, *N* banister-back chair, *O* Flemish chair, *P, Q, R* furniture hardware.

favored. Hood tops and shaped aprons were often used and softened the straight lines even more.

Much of the furniture was tall: beds, clocks, highboys, even the rounded top chair backs.

Decoration consisted of caning, lacquering (from the Orient) and veneering, which first began to be used widely. There still was carving, but inlay and marquetry proved more popular.

Colors were vigorous: strong reds, blues and greens in upholstery, along with gilding and lacquering, produced rich coloring against the paneled walls and dark furniture of which walnut was the principal wood.

## QUEEN ANNE

Queen Anne was the English sovereign from 1702 to 1714. The furniture style which carries her name reached its height of popularity in our country around 1720 to 1760 and is even today immensely popular.

The cyma curve (from the Greek meaning wave form or double curve) characterizes Queen Anne furniture. The artist William Hogarth (1697-1764) called the cyma curve "the line of beauty" and it is referred to by some as the "Hogarth curve." This term is particularly familiar to those of you who are flower arrangers.

The cyma curve is apparent in the familiar cabriole legs, chair backs, broken pediments, and skirt outlines, providing eye-pleasing curved lines to this comfortable furniture.

Chairs had upholstered slip seats, cabriole legs, either carved or plain and usually terminating with Dutch or pad feet, occasionally with ball and claw. The backs were either straight or spoon shaped for comfort, with a solid splat in the form of a vase or fiddle, thus giving rise to the common name of fiddle-back.

The all-upholstered chair was introduced for the first time in the form of the comfortable wing chair.

The rather plain highboys which appeared in the William and Mary furniture now became exquisite, tall, stately furniture, often topped with a broken arch pediment again in the familiar cyma curve. Lowboys, secretaries and corner cupboards were made, all with grace of line and simple in ornamentation.

Shells were the favorite carving ornament and appeared frequently on all kinds of furniture—knees of cabriole legs, cresting of chair backs, middle drawers and aprons of cabinet pieces—and was often seen as the central motif of carved designs.

Surfaces were for the most part plain without paneling or molding. Carving and ornamentation were simple in order not to detract from the beauty of line. Lacquer and veneer were used but inlay and marquetry passed out of fashion.

Walnut was the most-used wood, to the extent that Queen Anne is often called the "Age of Walnut." Curly maple was also popular in our country, and many fine examples are to be found in this decorative wood. Cherry, maple and gum were other woods used. Towards the end of the period, mahogany appeared although it was not used to any great extent.

Oriental rugs with rather large-scaled designs were the favorite floor-covering of the day. Chinese porcelains in soft colors, especially in blue and white, were much in favor as they harmonized nicely with the lacquered furniture. Bric-a-brac was abundant during this period and included Delft china and Venetian glass as well as Chinese porcelains. All these might be kept in mind for accessories and lamp bases in the modern home. (A word of caution to the amateur: do not attempt converting china or glass into a lamp base—this is a job for experts. Better still, buy your lamps as lamps already.)

Upholstery consisted of printed linen as well as much needlework. Needlepoint and crewelwork with the ever-popular tree of life design were favored; you might wish to make some yourself if your antiques need re-covering. Damasks and velvets were used, and Chinese wallpapers covered screens against the dark walnut walls. Brass fireplace accessories provided a warm contrast to the robust colors, which were dark, yet softened, shades of reds, blues, greens, copper and golds.

# QUEEN ANNE

A, B side chairs, B shows "spooned" back, C arm chair, D corner chair, E wing chair, F desk, G highboy, H lowboy, I, J tea tables, K tripod table, L brasses, M shell carving—a favorite ornament, N mirror, O cyma curves, P cabriole legs with club or pad foot.

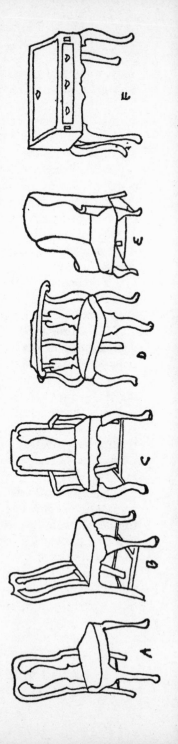

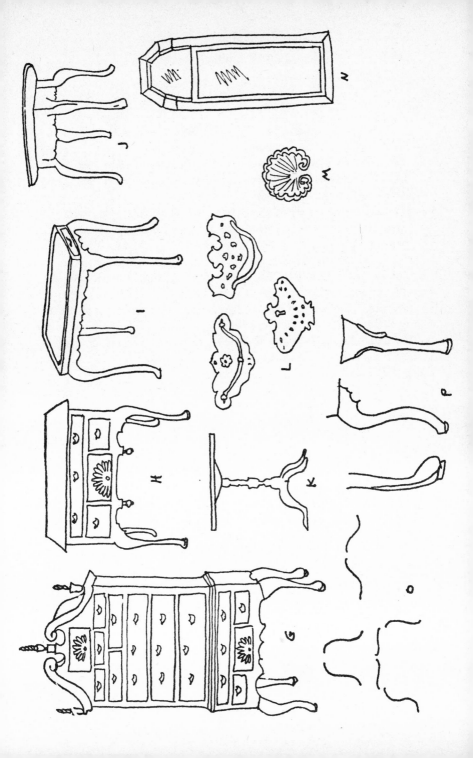

# CHIPPENDALE

Thomas Chippendale was an English cabinetmaker who lived from 1714 to 1779. A superb wood-carver and a master designer, he published a book of his designs in 1757 titled *The Gentleman and Cabinetmaker's Director*. The first book of its kind, the *Director* brought him world-wide fame.

Chippendale's styles are characterized by rich carving with the free use of curves. Graceful, beautiful and yet substantially proportioned furniture.

The ball and claw foot which is one of the most characteristic motifs associated with Chippendale was, strangely enough, not pictured in his book at all. Appearing on much Chippendale-style furniture, the ball and claw foot was used with cabriole legs. Other feet used with cabriole legs were club, web, and drake, but the ball and claw predominated. Bracket feet were used on some kinds of furniture, such as desks and chests of drawers.

Brasses were usually of the familiar "willow" shape.

There was a vogue for Chinese styles in England 1750-1765. The popularity of these Chinese styles current at that time prompted Chippendale to use Oriental motifs. The resultant designs evolved to become known as Chinese Chippendale, and featured straighter lines including the straight Malborough legs, the carved ladder-back chair and his carved fretwork.

Lacquered furniture, which was popular then, was elaborately decorated. Even such large pieces as highboys and chests-on-chests were lacquered in the Oriental manner.

Chippendale's furniture was beautifully designed and well built, so well, in fact, that much of what has remained is in excellent shape at present. His chairs were very strong structurally. All the Chippendale chair backs were fanciful, and are one of the highlights of his style. Even in the most delicate fretwork, care was taken to secure the maximum of strength: Instead of cutting a fret from one solid piece of wood, Chippendale's method was to cut three thicknesses ". . . which were glued together, the 'way' of the central thickness running in the opposite direction to the other two." This was obviously the forerunner to plywood, so much used today. (The actual invention of plywood is credited in 1854 to John Henry Belter, an American of German birth who had his shop in New York. Belter was issued a patent for it in 1856. Belter used 5-ply rosewood in the creation of his elaborate Victorian furniture.)

Wing chairs in Chippendale and Queen Anne styles are similar, thus often mistaken, one for the other. The chief difference lies in the construction of the arms: Queen Anne arms roll vertically and turn outward, while in the Chippendale style the roll is horizontal. Ball and claw feet are usually found on Chippendale wing chairs, but not always.

Mahogany was first discovered by Sir Walter Raleigh in 1595, but not used extensively until after 1720. Chippendale, as a talented wood carver, preferred mahogany, using it almost exclusively for his furniture.

Carving was of the finest quality, including such motifs as acanthus leaves, swags, shells, the "C" scroll, rococo shells, knotted ribbons, Georgian masks, hoofs, drake, and ball and claw feet.

Piecrust edges appeared on tables. Jigsaw mirrors, elaborate pediments on top of tall furniture, beautiful finials; all were characteristic of Chippendale. Highboys reached their peak of perfection during this period and bookcases became important for the first time.

The Chippendale-style furniture made in Philadelphia reached the climax of mahogany carving in America. The rival cabinetmakers seemed trying to outdo one another in design and execution of their fine examples as the elaborateness shows.

Philadelphia highboys and lowboys are unmatched in beauty of workmanship either here or in England. Richly carved feet, knees, skirts, central drawers of highboys and lowboys, quarter columns, frets, finials and cartouches were done in shells, scrolls, flowers, and other beautiful carving which sometimes was merely lines of beauty, rather than anything copied from nature, and surrounding the shell-like form in the center.

Although mahogany was the favorite wood of the period, there

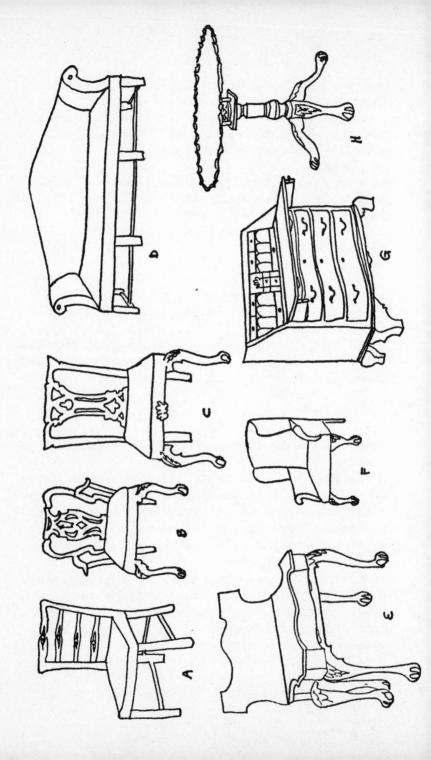

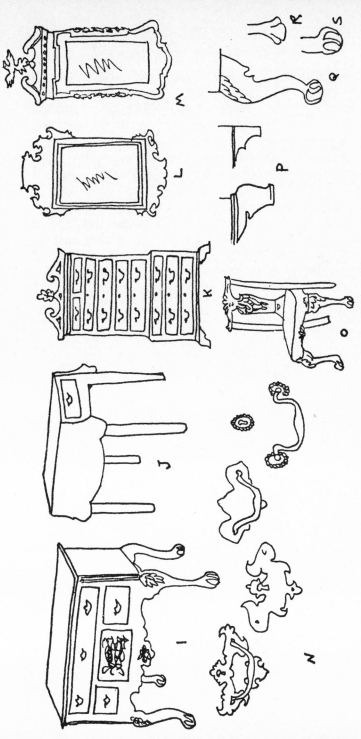

## CHIPPENDALE

*A, B, C* chairs, *D* sofa, *E* card table, *F* wing chair, *G* desk, *H* piecrust tripod table, *I* Philadelphia lowboy, *J* Pembroke table, *K* chest-on-chest, *L, M* mirrors, *N* Chippendale brasses, *O* ornately carved side chair, *P* bracket feet, *Q* cabriole leg with ball and claw foot, *R* drake foot, *S* ball and claw foot.

was furniture made of other woods. Some fine specimens are to be found in maple, cherry, and curly maple.

Colors favored were subtler in shade than those previously in vogue. Earlier colors were more robust, gradually becoming lighter to almost pastel shades by the end of the period. White painted walls were most popular, but the range of color seen was from light pearl to cream yellow to dark mulberry and various shades of brown.

Fabrics were usually rich and strong in color and bold in design; although in later years they tended toward subtler shades also. Cream, yellow, brown, and soft blue-green were most preferred. Patterned silks, damasks, brocades, brocatelles, velvets were used for upholstery. Needlepoint and tapestry were popular. Plain velvets were used for contrast with patterned materials.

The Chinese vogue made Chinese porcelains a favorite accessory used along with the china and glass from the preceding fashion.

## HEPPLEWHITE

George Hepplewhite, a London cabinetmaker, developed a style which found wide popularity. His influence was strongest from 1770 to 1790 and is still felt today.

After his death in 1786, his widow, Alice, continued his business and in 1788 she published a book of his furniture designs. The lightness and graceful elegance of his style were so well received that there were several more editions published at later dates.

Hepplewhite's style is distinguished by the light, straight leg forms, the serpentine fronts, refined curves, excellent inlay work and shield-back chairs.

Hepplewhite's chairs were not very strong structurally, often being found broken by the passage of time. They displayed great originality, being most usually the shield back, but also made with interlacing hearts and oval backs. The upholstery was carried down over the frame all around and finished with ornamental upholstery tacks.

Spade feet were a favorite of Hepplewhite, usually terminating square tapered legs. Round tapered legs with reeding or spiraling as preferred by Sheraton, were also used. Hepplewhite's straight legs differed from the Chinese Chippendale in that Hepplewhite's were tapered toward the foot, giving a light graceful line to even large, heavy pieces. For chests of drawers Hepplewhite used the French bracket foot with its curving skirt.

Sideboards came into being during this time and are associated with the Hepplewhite style. They are among the loveliest of his furniture.

Preferring veneer and inlay to carving, Hepplewhite-style furniture shows much beautiful inlay. He chose classic motifs for his furniture; the designs particularly distinctive of this style are wheat ears, pendant husks, bellflowers, round and oval paterae, and the Prince of Wales feathers. The fact that the Prince of Wales was one of his patrons of course increased Hepplewhite's reputation as a fine craftsman.

Mahogany was the most used wood, and rosewood, satinwood, tulipwood and other rare woods were employed for inlays.

Painting was another form of furniture adornment. Hepplewhite executed many commissions for the Adams Brothers (architects and furniture designers) and was in turn influenced by their designs, the free use of painting on furniture being one of their favorites.

Brasses for his furniture were round or oval.

Hepplewhite and Sheraton styles are very similar in many instances, in fact they used the same features so often that the styles are often difficult to tell apart. This is further complicated by the fact that what we consider to be Sheraton here in America is often called Hepplewhite in England, and vice versa.

Hepplewhite and Sheraton being contemporaries, their furniture and accessories shared the color preferences of their day.

Oriental rugs of small-scaled patterns were used as well as plain carpeting. Popular fabrics covered a wide range including silks, taffetas, velvets, brocades, chintzes, linens and cretonnes with bright, gay bird and flower patterns or such classic motifs as urns,

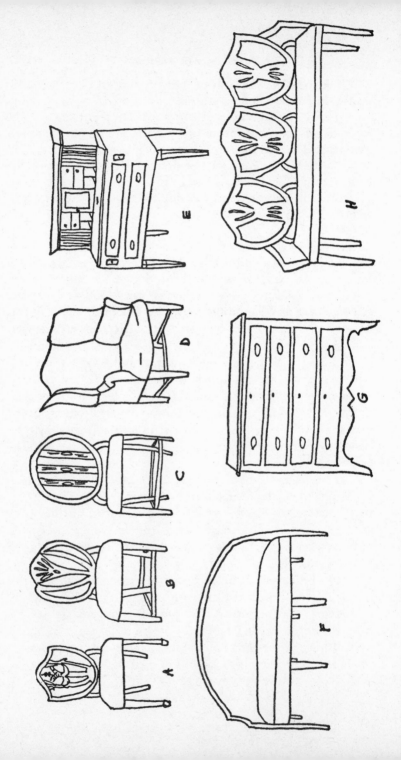

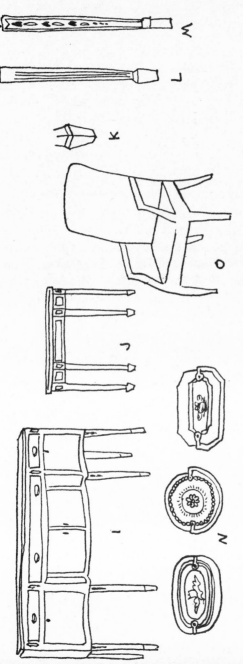

# HEPPLEWHITE

A, B, C side chairs, D wing chair, E tambour desk, F sofa, G chest of drawers, H settee, I sideboard, J table, K spade foot, L, M tapered Hepplewhite legs, N brasses, O Martha Washington chair.

swags, and flowers, all in small-scaled patterns. Festooning and French-style drapery were used for windows.

Muted, almost pastel colors were preferred along with formal arrangements. Gilt mirrors, Venetian glass, decorative porcelain such as Spode, Minton, Wedgwood, Sèvres, are all characteristic of the period. Classic shapes predominated.

# SHERATON

Thomas Sheraton (1750-1806) was an English cabinetmaker, drawing master, designer, publisher and preacher. All these activities kept him busy but barely earned him a living. He died a financial failure.

His designs were widely accepted, and they greatly influenced American furniture.

Sheraton style is characterized by square, straight-lined, solidly constructed furniture. Legs were slender, either round or square, tapering toward the turned, spade or block foot. Chair backs were square, often with a central panel rising slightly above the top rail; arms generally started high on the uprights and swept downward in an extended "S" shape to the supports which often were a continuation of the front legs. Stretchers were common, often "X" shaped, and part of the seat frame was allowed to show below the upholstery, a contrast to Hepplewhite's covered aprons.

Sheraton enjoyed detail and decorated his furniture wherever possible, leaving few plain surfaces. He used carving, inlay and painting. The painted fancy chair was exceedingly popular.

Mahogany was the preferred wood of the Sheraton style although such woods as satinwood, tulipwood, sycamore and rosewood for inlays were also used. Some of the woods used for veneers and inlays were stained to even richer colors than natural, and beautiful grains were chosen.

Decoration typical of Sheraton consisted of fluting, reeding, and spiral turning. Designs employed were lyre, urns, fan shaped and small ornamental disks, acanthus leaf, swags and stars.

Brasses were round, oval or hexagonal, and round glass knobs were used.

Toward the end of Sheraton's career the French Empire style had begun to appear and he made some furniture in this style. Due to this influence, later Sheraton furniture merges into Directoire and Empire styles, providing some confusion in attempting to define certain examples.

Hepplewhite and Sheraton styles overlap considerably in many instances and are difficult to tell apart at times. There were no copyrights at that time and furniture makers "borrowed" designs from each other regularly.

# SHERATON

*A, B, C, D* chairs, *E* sofa, *F, G* painted "fancy chairs," *H* chest of drawers, *I* card table, *J* sofa table, *K* chest with attached mirror, *L, M* sewing tables, *N* drum table, *O* bookcase desk (secretary), *P* bed, *Q* Constitution mirror, *R* Sheraton legs, *S* knob and brasses.

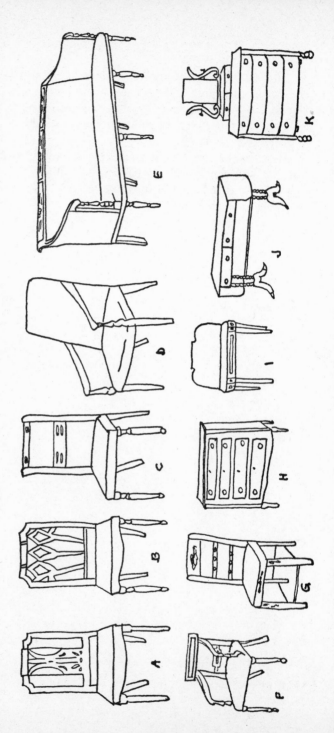

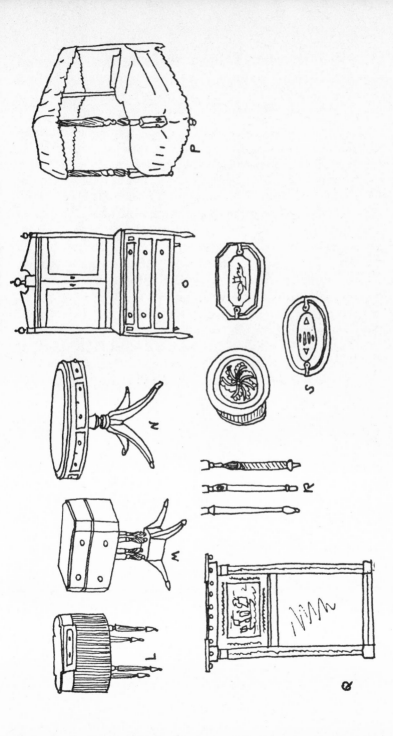

## DIRECTOIRE

After the Revolutionary War feelings were strong against England, and our new young country looked for designs toward France who had helped us in our fight for independence.

Directoire, popular from 1805-1815, was the forerunner to French Empire fashions. Napoleon had been made Emperor in 1804 and desired martial, spartan and patriotic motifs. His time abroad inspired the neo-classic motifs with Egyptian and Roman decorations.

Directoire is noted for its saber-leg sofas (so called because of their resemblance to cavalry swords), Grecian couches, curule legs, lyre-back chairs and forward curving chair legs.

Mahogany was still the preferred wood and was often carved. Mahogany paneling was used for walls.

Neo-classic decorative designs were employed. They included wreaths, laurel branches, lyres, stars, rosettes, urns, palm leaves, as well as the more martial designs of battle axes, torches and shields.

Patriotic colors of red, white and blue were very popular in our country along with the American bald eagle. The more typical colors for Directoire, however, are terra cotta, orange, dull chocolate brown, blue-green, green-black, and yellow-green. Painted furniture was often soft grey or beige.

Striped fabrics and small delicate patterns were used. Toile de Jouy cottons were a favorite fabric.

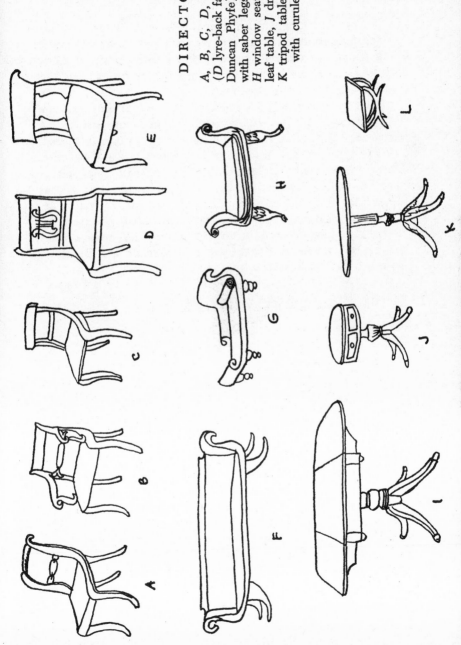

## DIRECTOIRE

A, B, C, D, E chairs (D lyre-back favored by Duncan Phyfe), F sofa with saber legs, G sofa, H window seat, I drop-leaf table, J drum table, K tripod table, L stool with curule legs.

## DUNCAN PHYFE

A New York cabinetmaker, Duncan Phyfe (1795-1856) made fashionable furniture for the carriage trade of his day. His finest work was done from 1800 to 1820. Phyfe made much furniture, but not nearly as much as has been attributed to him. No one man could have possibly made that much.

There is no actual "Duncan Phyfe" in itself, although his fine interpretations of what was currently popular gave rise to the erroneous calling of all furniture done in those styles by his name.

The styles he did make were late Sheraton and Directoire. There was so much similarity and overlapping of styles during that time that it is simpler and less confusing to class these various designs together and call them Early Empire, as is often done.

A fine cabinetmaker, Phyfe's well-constructed, tastefully executed furniture declined in artistry as the later Empire styles became fashionable. His earlier pieces in Sheraton and Directoire styles were in much better taste.

## AMERICAN EMPIRE

American Empire (1815-1840) is a distinctly different version of the French Empire, being a much less ornate form. Carving on American pieces took the place of the French brass and ormolu mounts, and there was less gilding.

Painting remained popular in the decoration of chairs; the tremendous popularity of the painted fancy chair is testified to by the fact that by 1826 Lambert Hitchcock was turning out fifteen thousand chairs of this type annually, and there were other factories producing similar chairs at the same time.

Empire furniture was heavy and massive, and is considered by many as being decadent and the end of good furniture.

It is characterized by acanthus leaves, pineapples, animal paw feet, heavy cornices and lion's head brasses. The beautiful mahogany used, and the fine carving were highlights of the style. Other woods were used, curly maple among them. Mahogany remained the favorite wood but was often used in combination with veneers of either tiger-striped maple or bird's-eye maple. Crotch mahogany was also used frequently.

Typical of Empire furniture were sleigh beds, sofas with cornucopia legs or winged feet, bear claw feet often terminated carved columns on chests or other case pieces, pineapples were almost always used for finials, heavy tables with pineapple or lyre pedestals, and ogee mirrors. Late in the period heavy, scrolled legs appeared.

Hardware consisted of round wooden knobs for some furniture, round brass knobs for other, while the more ornate exhibited lion's head brasses with ring pulls.

Dull brown, deep blues and greens, including emerald green, predominated the color schemes although terra cotta, white, mauve, apricot pink and gray were also used. Fabrics featured large-scaled patterns and Egyptian and Roman motifs.

# EMPIRE

A, B, C chairs, D, E, I sofas, F pedestal table, H, J chests of drawers, K sideboard, L sleigh bed, M, N carved animal feet, O, P, Q acanthus leaf, cornucopia, pineapple—favorite carvings, R knobs and brasses, S ogee mirror, T secretary.

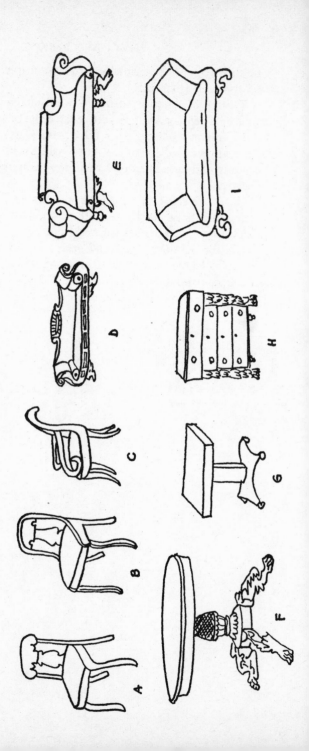

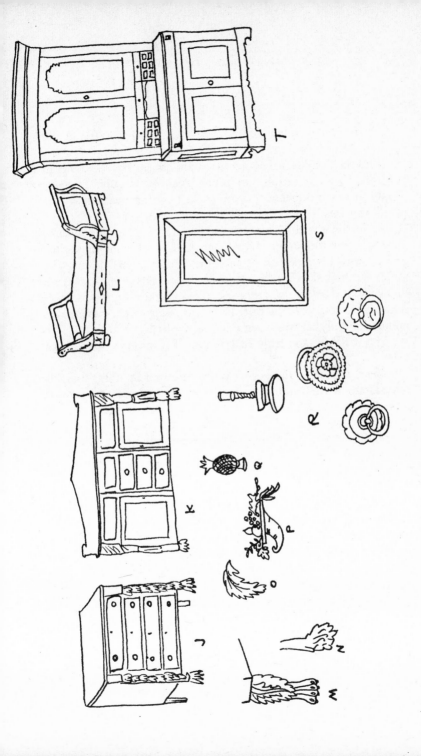

## VICTORIAN

Queen Victoria reigned in England from 1837 to 1901, giving her name to the furniture fashionable during that time.

With the domination of television and its endless Westerns in our lives, Victorian settings are brought into view daily. To many people this is the mental picture evoked by the mention of the word "antiques."

With the advent of modern mechanical tools, a change came upon the furniture scene. Like sister with a new pinking shears, or Dad with his new power-tools, the cabinetmakers of the Victorian era desired to try their new "toys" on everything available. Fretwork, curlycues, and fancyness appeared on everything. Dust-catching crevices were the rule. Inlay had disappeared, carving was minimized and that was often done by machine.

The machine age truly had begun. The machine had taken over.

The first part of the period is characterized by ugly, straight-lined Gothic-style furniture. Later, however, this eyesore was over-taken by the graceful curves of a more attractive style, adapted from French designs.

Marble tops were frequently used on commodes, chests of drawers and tables. Marble is generally thought of in connection with Victorian furniture since it was used so often, although marble tops were used on some Empire hall tables and even as far back as Queen Anne. The *Maryland Gazette,* a newspaper of Annapolis, Maryland, carried an advertisement for "Imported marble top tables" in its issue of January 9, 1761.

Walnut was once again the most favored wood, and pieces made of pine were often stained to resemble walnut. Mahogany and rosewood were also used, as well as pine, maple and cherry.

Among the furniture were such handy items as wash stands, dry sinks, commodes, towel stands, hideous hall racks, and small chests of drawers. Massive wooden beds were characteristic of the style although in rural districts short posts and trundle beds were made.

Metal furniture appeared in several forms, including the familiar ice-cream chairs and metal beds. Amid the twisted metal, brass beds appeared, sturdy and gleaming.

Furniture was often made in sets such as this one advertised in a Philadelphia newspaper in November of 1874:

Gould & Co., Philadelphia, Pa.
Christmas Presents and New-Years Gifts
This SOLID WALNUT, Italian Marbletop Chamber suit,
containing nine (9) separate pieces,
will be packed free and shipped to
any part of the World on receipt of
FIFTY-THREE DOLLARS ($53)
Every other conceivable description of
Furniture at equally low prices.

N.E. cor. Market & 9th Sts.
242 & 244 South Second St.
87 & 89 North Second St.
272 South Second St.
and
1206 Market St.
Philadelphia, Pa.

Complete sets such as those advertised, and much other furniture, were made to be sold together. Gentleman's and Lady's chairs, chairs and sofas, bedroom suites, and parlor "suits" were typical.

Love seats were frequently seen and captain's chairs were mass produced.

What-nots were extremely popular and much bric-a-brac was used to fill them. Colorful cranberry glass was sold cheaply in variety stores and through mail-order houses. Witch balls, those useless blown glass balls, were often seen. Much ornate glassware in fancy shapes was popular during Victorian times—these are now referred to as "art glass."

Britannia ware, the first cousin to pewter, was used.

Drawer pulls were in the form of wooden handles, carved (usually by machine) in leaf, or fruit and leaf patterns.

# VICTORIAN

A, B, C, D chairs, E, F sofas, G, H tables, I student's desk, J commode, K chest with attached mirror, L marble-top chest of drawers, M, N wash stands, O, P whatnots, Q marble-top table, R bed, S wooden knobs, T rocking chair, U Gone-With-the-Wind lamp, V glass lamp, W parlor suite.

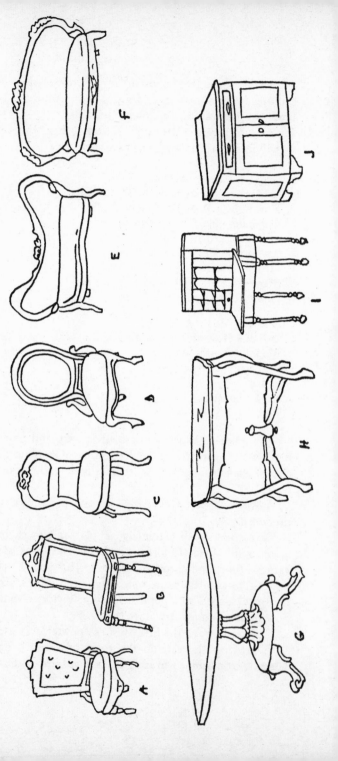

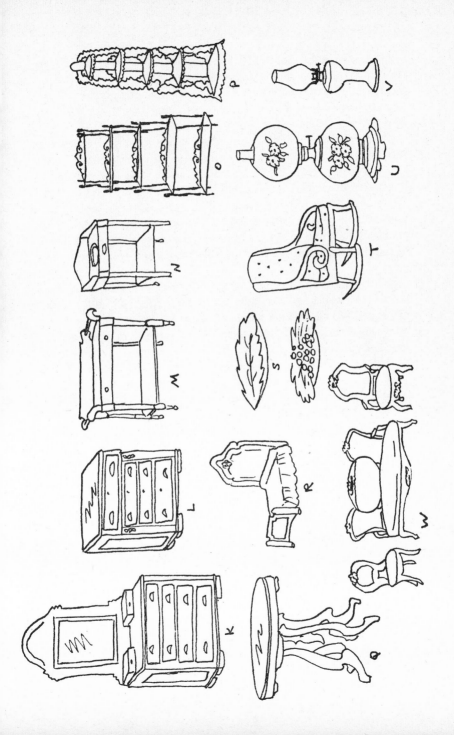

The so-called "Gone-With-the-Wind" lamps were in vogue as well as taller stately banquet lamps, student lamps and the plainer glass kerosene lamps. Swinging-arm, cast iron bracket lamps were produced literally by hundreds of thousands from 1875 to 1910.

In rural sections of the country some of the simpler forms of furniture in pine, maple and cherry were still being made with hand tools and by the same methods as earlier. This is often called "Victorian Provincial" or "Primitive" furniture, and includes such pieces as six-board chests, chests of drawers with bootjack ends, wash stands, Welsh dressers, commodes and simple tables. These pieces are not high in value as far as intrinsic values go, but some of the better examples are delightfully quaint and well worth collecting.

Colors most favored during the Victorian era include all the purples, as well as mauve, lilac, lavender, pink, baby blue, dark green and brown. Rooms were often painted in deep colors with light woodwork. Wallpaper usually had large floral patterns as did the rugs.

Fabrics were heavy and elegant. Elaborate lace curtains were used either alone or with heavy draperies which were deeply fringed; curtains at doorways were tied back. For upholstery, black horsehair was most typical although other colors and colored satin and brocatelle as well as plain velvets were used almost as much. Tables were always covered, often with heavy, floor-length fabrics.

A great deal of accessories and bric-a-brac was displayed, and the rooms appeared crowded.


## COUNTRY FURNITURE

What is meant by the terms "country made" or "provincial" is just that the furniture in question was constructed in one of the more rural areas as opposed to the large centers of manufacture. This does not imply poorer construction, for the furniture was just as well constructed; but rather more simplified forms than were being made in Philadelphia, Baltimore or Newport. The differences can be compared with French Provincial, which was the more simplified forms of Louis XV and Louis XVI.

Country furniture often includes such items as butterfly tables, gateleg tables, simple pembroke tables, etc.

In those days, as at present, there were some customers who preferred less elaborate ornamentation, less carving and no inlay, as well as the correspondingly lower prices. Some splendid examples of antique furniture fall in this category: furniture which is more in keeping with today's casual living than the more elaborate specimens with their wealth of detail and imported woods.

Simplicity of line was paramount. Fancy grained woods were often used to substitute for carving and inlay. The woods most used were pine, maple, cherry, curly maple, apple, pear and birch.

## PRIMITIVES

Country furniture of the simplest kinds, made with hand tools, and of native woods (usually pine, maple and cherry) with plain hardware are generally called primitives.

These pieces are often quaint, some to the point of crudity.

## ROCKING CHAIRS

The rocking chair is strictly an American innovation, our own Benjamin Franklin often being credited with the invention.

The first rocking chairs were made by adding rockers to regular chairs. This has been done often since, and there are usually a few converted chairs of this type around.

Rocking chairs have been made in many styles; the most popular was the Boston rocker which was made in quantity from the 1820's to 1890. This familiar chair is characterized by its rolled and scrolled seat, its wide top rail so often decorated, and its extreme comfort.

## WINDSOR CHAIRS

Originating in England in the 1500's, Windsor chairs became a great favorite here in America and were made in vast amounts.

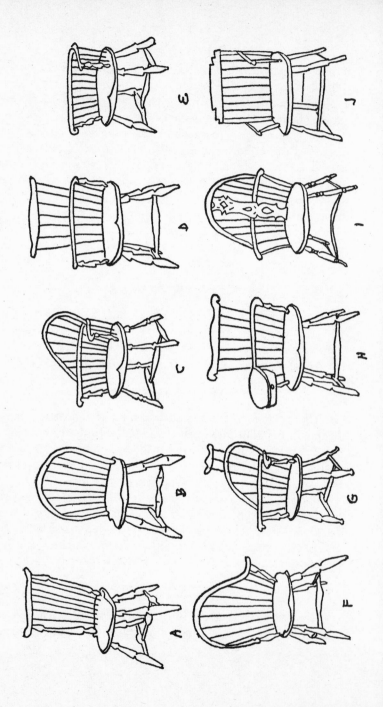

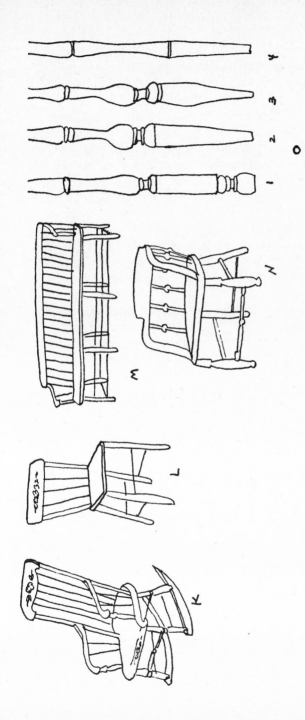

# WINDSOR CHAIRS

*A* fan back, *B* hoop back, or bow back, *C* hoop-back armchair, *D* comb back, *E* low-back Windsor, *F* bow back with one-piece bow and arms, *G* triple back-comb on top of bow back, *H* writing arm, *I* English Windsor with splat in back, *J* straight back—Sheraton influence, *K* Boston rocker, *L* late Windsor (not desirable), *M* Windsor settee, *N* captains chair—late, *O* Windsor turnings: *1* Philadelphia, *2* general New England, *3* Rhode Island and *4* Bamboo turnings.

from 1725 up to, and including, today. English forms vary from ours, particularly in that their versions have a splat in the middle of the back while ours are composed of all spindles.

The popularity of Windsor chairs was always high because these simple wooden chairs are attractive as well as comfortable. Records show that both George Washington and Thomas Jefferson ordered Windsors in quantity, Jefferson referring to them by the English name of "stick chairs." These comfortable chairs have graced the White House as well as numberless humble cottages all over our country.

Very old Windsors were made partly of seasoned and partly of unseasoned woods; thus insuring added strength to the finished chair, for when the green wood dried it shrank, grabbing tightly to the already seasoned parts, forming a stronger bond than could be effected by glue.

Several woods were used in their construction: Hickory for hoops, ash or hickory for spindles, pine for seats, and maple or birch for the legs. These were usually painted, and all colors have been found, but the particular favorite was green.

Many forms of Windsor chairs were made. The rarest and most valuable is the writing arm Windsor, followed by the three-backed chair.

The earlier and better examples had deeply shaped seats and well-splayed legs. Later, seats became squarer and there was less splay to the legs. Very late Windsors deteriorated into the plank-seat, arrow-back chairs which bear little resemblance to stately Windsor and are not considered to be Windsor chairs at all. Another debased form is known as the captain's chair.

Other forms of Windsors include the Boston rocker and the mammy benches, which were so long that they were sold by the foot (records show that Hitchock charged forty cents per foot).

A fine Windsor chair is a welcome addition to any room.*

---

* Wallace Nutting covered the subject of Windsor chairs well. His pictures and comments are recommended.

# BLOCK FRONT FURNITURE

Considered by many to be the finest furniture ever made, the shell-carved block fronts showed excellent construction, beautiful design and superb carving.

John Goddard (1724-1785), a cabinetmaker of note in Newport, Rhode Island, invented the block front and had fifteen children—quite an accomplishment for any man. Several of his sons became cabinetmakers as was also his father-in-law, Job Townsend.

Three blocks help form the contour of the front of this furniture: the middle one concave, and those to either side convex. In good examples the whole drawer front is made of one plank which had to be 3 inches thick to accommodate the carving.

Where shell carving appeared, the top board was straight, but where the block front was plain the top board was of a similar contour to the front.

Goddard developed a particularly lovely bracket foot of the ogee type.

Desks, both flat top and fall front, secretaries, chests of drawers and chests-on-chests were made during the rather short period of 1750 to 1780.

Mahogany was the usual wood, although there were occasional examples made in maple and cherry.

It is truly a shame that there were not more of these magnificent specimens made, for there are few available today.

# PENNSYLVANIA DUTCH

Chests of the simple board construction were a great favorite for they could be decorated with the jolly, colorful paintings which were so much a part of the people called Pennsylvania Dutch. Other pieces of furniture, as well as the houses and barns, were gayly painted with symbolic patterns.

Fat little hearts, peacocks and other colorful birds, unicorns, stars within circles, and—most of all—tulips, appear in gay profusion amid riots of color.

A

B

C

D

E

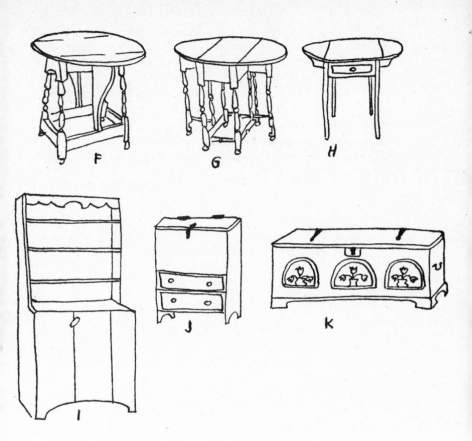

# BLOCK FRONTS AND MISCELLANEOUS

*A* Block front secretary, *B* Block front chest, *C* slat-back chair, *D* shaving mirror,
*E* settle, *F* butterfly table, *G* gate-leg table, *H* Pembroke table, *I* Welsh dresser,
*J* blanket chest, *K* Pennsylvania Dutch decorated chest.

Much furniture was initialed and some dated. Dower chests especially were elaborately painted with the name of the bride and the date being prominent. These are much sought-after examples, for all too often the decorations have been painted over by some later owner, or worn off.

The paintings are primitive in character yet carefully executed; the colors gay and bright. So popular were their designs that even today we are copying them.

# Attic Antiques

## OBSOLETE

THERE ARE NUMEROUS OLD ITEMS which have not yet attained the age of "antique" yet which are very old, not being made any more, and often obsolete. Just as old automobiles are called antique cars despite their relatively young age, so, too, are these many old things referred to as antiques.

Under this encompassing category comes much old furniture which has been relegated to the attic. Dusty, cobwebby relics of the past, they bring nostalgic memories of our grandparents.

## GONE-WITH-THE-WIND LAMPS

So prevalent in the 1890s, they are covered in Chapter 8.

## DOUGH TRAYS

Dough trays, or dough boxes, are usually of pine. They were apparently made both with the addition of legs and just as a plain box-like article. Often the addition of legs was a later development, sometimes attractive, and sometimes otherwise. The main requirements for the skirt and legs is that they be in good proportion and nicely splayed (placed on an angle with the feet spread further out than where they join the furniture.)

These covered wooden boxes were used to hold dough during the rising period, just as today you place your yeast dough in a closed cupboard with a bowl of hot water to provide the right environment for proper rising. The removable top of the dough tray was a handy place to knead and roll out the dough into loaves and rolls.

Today dough trays with legs are used as lamp tables or end tables. The interior provides a storage place for odds and ends.

## DRY SINKS

Made as late as the 1890's, these are usually of pine, the sink part sometimes found lined with tin. Both large and small examples were made and serve useful purposes today: in the kitchen, dining room or in the foyer.

The tin-lined sink can be filled with potted plants surrounded by sphagnum moss, or they can be used as a gardening center as mentioned in Chapter 3.

Dry sinks are more at home in a casual atmosphere and look out of place amid fine inlay and carving of the more formal house.

## CHAIRS

Plank seat chairs, arrow back chairs, captain's chairs are all to be found in plentiful quantity. Not particularly desirable in themselves, when in sturdy condition they can be refinished either in natural color or painted and make useful additions to any household.

## WAGON SEATS

Best when used for game rooms, patios or gardens. Without added legs they can be used in children's rooms, but legs will be necessary to bring them up to comfortable seating height for adults.

## COBBLERS' BENCHES

A lowly form of furniture, these hardly belong in the house unless the owner has a sense of humor and wishes to pep up a basement bar.

Again for the patio or garden, it will make a convenient coffee table.

With so much antique furniture to choose from, it is unnecessary to employ such crudities as cobblers' benches for furniture.

## APOTHECARY ITEMS

In the days before the dark, mysterious Apothecary Shops, the home-made remedies used were frequently as horrible as the diseases which they were supposed to cure. Here are a few actively used in 1671:

Receipt for the Scratches.
One quart fishworms, washed clean, one pound hog's lard stewed together; filtered through a strainer and add one-half pint of oil of turpentine, one half pint good brandy. Simmer it well and it is fit for use.

(Well, at least the worms were washed and the brandy good.)

For ye toothe ache.
Take a little piece of opium as big as a great pinnes head and put it into the hollow place of the Akeing Toothe and it will guie pleasant Ease.

This remedy is followed by the reassuring note, "Often tryed by me apon many People and never fayled."

By 1896 patent medicines had overshadowed the do-it-yourself remedies as seen in the newspaper and magazine advertisements of that date. One such advertisement offers:

No matter how painful the disease or of how long standing, if taken as directed, "5DROPS" will always cure.

(What will it cure, you wonder? Well the ad continues . . .)

Rheumatism, Sciatica, Neuralgia, Dyspepsia, Backache, Asthma, Hay Fever, Catarrh, Sleeplessness, Nervousness, Nervous and Neuralgic Headaches, Heart Weakness, Toothache, Earache, Croup, La Grippe, Malaria, Creeping Numbness, Bronchitis, and kindred diseases, one and all quickly and permanently yield to this almost magical medicine.

Other advertisements in the same periodical also had cures for all common ailments from overweight to falling hair. Even love charms and eye glasses by mail were among the classified sections in the "good old days," and Lydia E. Pinkham had the answer to all of woman's troubles.

As the drug stores of their day, the Apothecary Shops were dim and gloomy places where portions of skeletons hung from the ceiling. Great parchment books, bellows and hour glasses were prominent and mortars and pestles were indispensable. Cobwebs and dust were frequent decorations over all else.

The varied and interestingly shaped bottles which were so important then are collected today. The largest bottles can be used for cookie jars, and the smaller sizes for anything from candy to whatever the size and shape suggests to you. Those previously used for medicines must be thoroughly cleaned before using of course.

Apothecary chests contain many drawers, usually equal rows of square drawers. These roomy chests are wonderful for catchalls to store many things conveniently. They can be used in almost any room so long as they harmonize with the furniture already there. In a bedroom, the multitudinous drawers provide storage for out-of-season sweaters, scarves, and woolens during the summer; and for bathing suits, shorts, tee-shirts, sandals and summer clothing during the cold weather. In the dining room, they can hold silver, silver polish, furniture polish, frogs, needlepoint holders, floral clay, candles, cheese board, wooden salad bowls, place mats, napkins, or anything that does not have a place of its own. In the kitchen, the Apothecary chests are useful for storing smaller pots, lids, extra light bulbs, cookie press, cake decorater set, and the less-often-used utensils.


## ICE-CREAM CHAIRS

Recently there has been considerable interest in Victorian ice-cream chairs and their matching tables. Painted a cheerful color, they have a charming old-fashioned appearance with the ability to be usable where space is limited.

Two ice-cream chairs and a tiny table will often fit into a corner of a small kitchen or into an alcove, to provide a cosy breakfast nook, a place for a quick lunch or coffee-break, a quiet corner to

figure out the week's menus, sort your recipes, balance your check-
book before Husband sees it, or a good place to set up the checkerboard for junior and his little friend. In your basement recreation
room the ice-cream chairs can be the decorating spark to a very
attractive room.

Comfortable around the barbecue pit or for the patio, they
should be brought inside during inclement weather.


## SEA CHESTS

These low chests with their rounded lids can be used for
storage of blankets or out-of-season clothing.

The hallway, if it is wide enough, is a good place for one of
these; or a stair landing, again if space permits.

A framed seascape or whaling scene would look very good
hanging above.


## SPINNING WHEELS

There are two kinds of spinning wheels: the large wool wheel
and the smaller flax wheel. Not actually a piece of furniture,
still, it is used as decoration in the house. It is difficult to determine the age of a spinning wheel, for they were made and used
over such a long expanse of time.

Small flax wheels are often placed near the fireplace. The
larger wool wheels take up more space even though they are so
narrow. One of the most effective places in which we have seen
one displayed is at the top landing of a stairway, where it can
be seen from the floor below and also from the street, since there is
a window on the landing. Another attractive place would be in
front of a picture window.


## TABLES AND CHESTS

All sorts of tables and chests of dubious age are to be found.
It will be best to take time to look them over very carefully, for it
might well be that what does not look like much at first may be

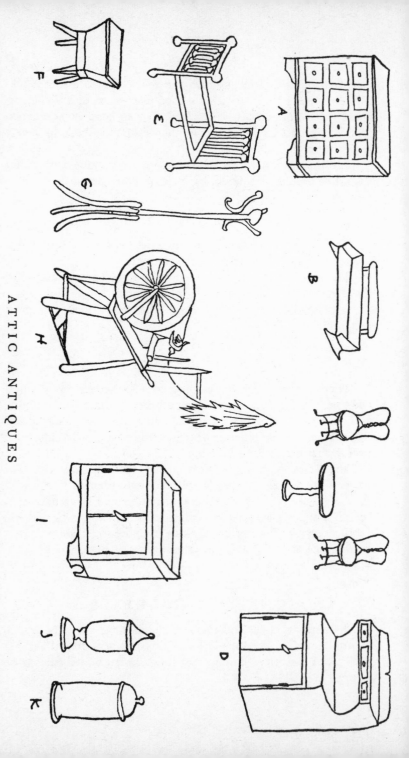

ATTIC ANTIQUES

A apothecary chest, B wagon seat, C ice-cream chairs and table, D dry sink, E brass bed, F dough tray, G hall tree, H spinning wheel, I dry sink, J, K apothecary bottles.

valuable after all. One such discovery was made by a couple searching for a hanging cabinet for their kitchen. They chanced across what seemed to be a very old cabinet, but they could not tell exactly because it had been painted all over even to the glass in the door, and had been used as a medicine chest in a basement. They liked the shape of the piece and took a chance, buying it for five dollars. After they had removed the paint they discovered, much to their pleasure, that eleven of the twelve tiny panes of glass were the original hand blown glass and that the wood was curly maple.

Search for signs of age in construction, style, period, hardware and finish. Develop your eye for spotting pleasing line and good style, so that you will be able to find that one good article hiding amid all the junk. One good "find" will overbalance a hundred disappointments and is well worth the effort.

## PAINTED CHINA

The hand-painted china that our grandmother loved so much is scorned by most antique collectors. True, it hasn't the age nor the sophistication to be accredited as such, and yet much of it has merit. The soft coloring and the naturalistic flowers endear themselves to most women. Extra china is always useful in any household, and painted china has a second feature to recommend it—it can be so effectively displayed in china cabinets or on open Welsh dressers. Used this way, it can add the accent color to a room. The larger plates can be hung on the wall with plate hangers that do not show, thus giving the appearance of a round picture.

When choosing hand-painted china, look first of all for artistically good painting, colors you most prefer, and of course for good china as the base.

# Antiques Other Than Furniture

## LAMPS AND LIGHTING

IsN'T IT ANNOYING when a fuse blows! You have to fumble around in the dark looking for the flashlight and go out into the kitchen, or even worse, way down into the basement to put in that new fuse. This task amounts to about the same amount of effort as unscrewing and replacing the cap to a tube of toothpaste. A murmured sigh of satisfaction escapes your lips with the return of the lights and the sound of the radio once again. You flip off the flashlight and mumble something about, "Why doesn't someone invent something so we can avoid this sort of thing!" Blown fuses *are* annoying even if they only occur occasionally.

But, think how much more annoying was the constant tending required of oil lamps: cleaning, filling, rewicking, picking up the wick, trimming the wick, adjusting the flame, refilling. The total result was flickering light which was often sooty and always evil smelling.

The history of lighting is one of the most fascinating of all the antique-to-modern developments.

The very first lights were from fires. After man had conquered fire he discovered that it was an excellent source of light in those dark hours past sundown, and began a long series of attempts to produce this light for his purposes.

Fire has been the chief kind of light ever since, taking many forms to keep it going from many kinds of oil and animal fat, and including such familiar forms as candles and our present-day lighting of street obstructions with the round, fat little open flame markers lined up around the danger area.

The first actual lamp was little more than a concave stone or a crudely shaped metal vessel to hold meat drippings and a little floating wick.

The Betty lamp was an improved version of the grease lamp and continued in use over a tremendously long time. Starting some time around 6000 B.C., these lamps were used in the same form A.D. 1620 when our country was first being settled. The little cloth wicks merrily burned their feeble lights in countless grease-filled Betty lamps for many generations of Americans, in designs hardly different from those used by the early Romans. There was a patent issued to a Lancaster, Pennsylvania, firm as late as March 13, 1860, for a Betty lamp, which shows that they were probably used into the 1870's.

By far the most widely used fuel for lamps was whale oil. The great whaling industry was flourishing along the coast and whale oil had a less obnoxious odor than the lard which was also burned during the same period.

Made of several materials including tin, iron and pewter, whale-oil lamps may be easily distinguished by their little wick tubes: small round wick tubes for the whale oil in sharp contrast to the broad, flat ones for lard oil.

Similar in shapes were the lamps that burned camphene. This fluid was a product of refined turpentine which was in general use from about 1845 to 1850. Unlike whale or lard oil, camphene was highly explosive, therefore, the wick tubes were made longer to prevent the flame from getting into the oil font. Also, camphene lamps had tight-fitting brass caps attached to the wick tubes by tiny chains; these little caps were used to extinguish the lamp because the usual method of blowing out a lamp as for whale oil, was too dangerous with explosive camphene.

Many varied and interestingly collectable shapes can be found in lamps of all these kinds.

The lamp used on sailing vessels is called a gimbel lamp, and has a unique construction to allow it to swing with the movement of the ship, yet never be in danger of tipping over in rough seas. Not many of these remain today.

Sometime around 1810 or so, came the invention of wick tubes on a disk which was in turn cemented onto a cork in order to fit

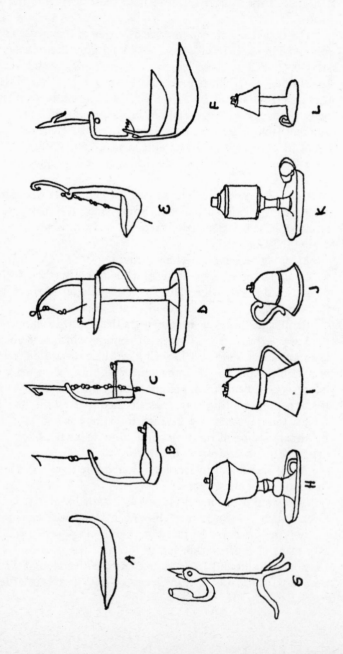

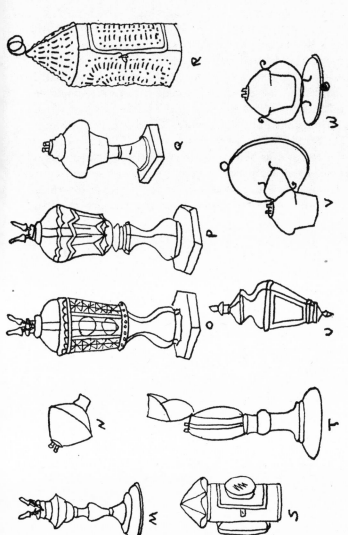

# LIGHTING

*A* open grease lamp, *B, C, D, E* Betty lamps (*D* Betty lamp on a stand), *F* Phoebe lamp, *G* rush light holder, *H, I, J, K, L* whale-oil lamps, *M* camphene lamp, *N* peg lamp—to fit candlestick, *O, P* glass camphene lamps, *Q* glass whale-oil lamp, *R* pierced tin lantern, *S* tin oil lantern, *T* bull's-eye lamp, *U* carriage lamp, *V, W* used aboard ships, the gimble lamp remained upright at all times, could be set on table or hung on wall.

into the neck of a glass lamp. These are usually found with the cork part missing. Soon following these were other glass lamps that were made with a threaded brass neck for the wick holders.

Kerosene was found to be a superior fuel for lighting although still far from Mr. Edison's wonderful incandescent bulb. In 1793 M. Argand, a Swiss chemist from Geneva, invented a round burner with holes in the side through which more air was drawn against the flame, making it a steadier and brighter light. This burner was an epoch-making contribution to the development of lighting. All subsequent oil lamps made were based upon this principle.

From around 1875 kerosene came into general usage as a lighting fuel. Lamps were made in huge quantities and in unlimited sizes and shapes. Extensively used, kerosene lamps were subject to style and as late as the May 1906 issue of the *Ladies' Home Journal* there was an illustrated article showing "Good and Bad Taste in Lamps." The Standard Oil Company advertised "The Rayo Lamp" in 1907, describing it as being "made of brass throughout, beautifully nickled. Every lamp warranted."

These lamps can be put to practical usage if you collect them today. Filled with kerosene they serve their original purpose when used for outdoor summer evening illumination for your patio, for camping trips, for the beach cottage, or the hunting lodge.

Simple electric "adapters" are available at a nominal cost to convert kerosene lamps into electric lamps. All you have to do is to unscrew the burner and replace it with the electrified one which looks much the same except for the electric cord; even the chimney remains to give an authentic appearance.

The so called "Gone-With-the-Wind" lamps actually date from around the 1890's until the 1920's. Originally called "parlor lamps," they received their commonly used name from their erroneous use in the motion picture of the book by that name. The dates of manufacture seem indecently late for items generally thought of as antique; yet they are obsolete, and so colorful that the ages can be brushed aside as unimportant after a casual mention in passing. Once electrified, these fancy lamps are used effectively with many of the later styles of antiques and have the obvious advantage of giving good light. Occasionally these are seen electrified in both top and bottom; the bottoms, of course, never gave light originally, as that portion was the receptacle for the kerosene.

Besides lamps, there were other forms of lighting, one of the crudest being the burning of certain portions of the pitch pine tree, usually the fleshy roots and pine knots. It is said that Abraham Lincoln studied his lessons by the fireplace to which he added pine knots for extra light. When burned, they give off a bright, clear light, sufficient for reading.

Candles were made at home by one of two long processes. First tallow was purified by boiling with water, the fat rose to the top and was skimmed off; this process was repeated several times before dipping wicks in and out until candles were formed. The wicks were tied, several to a long stick, for dipping at one time, then the stick was placed over the backs of two chairs while another batch was being dipped; these are the candle sticks referred to in the old nursery rhyme, "Jack be nimble, Jack be quick, Jack jump over the candle stick." The other method of making candles was by the use of a mold. The tallow was poured into the mold in which the wicks had already been placed. Tin candle molds of many sizes are still to be found. They were made in numerous sizes to mold from one to as many as two dozen candles at a time. Through curiosity on the part of the author it was discovered that it is possible to make nice candles without previous experience by using these molds. Glass vials inserted into candle molds make interesting flower containers for hanging on the wall, or for a tall shelf.

Candlesticks were made in iron, brass, pewter, britannia, tin, silver and glass in many pleasing shapes from plain iron "hog scrapers" to elegant solid silver. The first candlesticks had a pricket on which the candle was impaled, later came the socket type which is in use today. The short, broad-based candlesticks are called chamber candlesticks since their safety from dripping wax made them excellent for use in the bed chamber.

Every house needs candlesticks both for the table and for emergency light during power failures. There are so many lovely candlesticks available that you will have no trouble finding just the kind that will look best in your house.

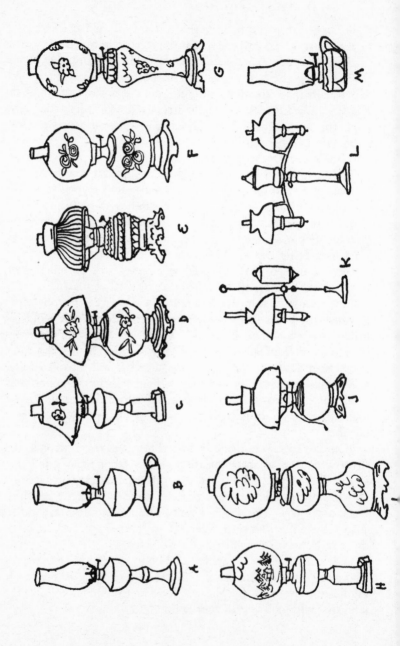

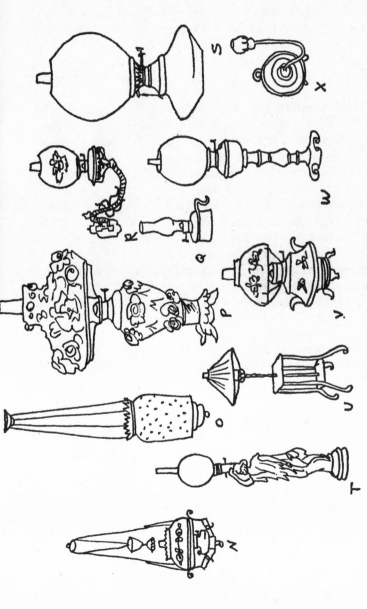

## MORE LIGHTING

A, B, C glass kerosene lamps, D, E, F, G, H, I, J parlor lamps (F called Gone-With-the-Wind lamp), K, L student's lamps, M glass lamp, N, O hanging lamps, P fancy "pickle jar" lamp, Q miniature "Nutmeg" lamp, R cast-iron bracket lamp, S advertised as a plain lamp for home decoration, T figure based lamp, U table lamp 1900, V kerosene parlor lamp, W banquet lamp, X "Little Beauty" night lamp.

Candle sconces were attractive ways to increase the feeble one-candlelight illumination. The sconce is a fixture for holding a candle or candles with a reflective surface back of it; these were made of several materials and frequently had bits of mirror or polished tin fastened on decoratively. Usually hung on the wall, they were often of such design that they could also be set upon a table.

Candles were expensive and troublesome to make, yet candlesticks were often so lovely that in order to use them even without using candles, the peg lamp was invented. This was a glass oil lamp which terminated, not in the usual base, but instead in a small peg which would fit into the candlestick, thus giving this particular lamp its descriptive name.

Hurricane glasses are just stately, tall glass cylinders open at both ends and bulging in the middle. They are 20″ to 30″ tall and are placed over the lighted candlesticks to keep the light steady and protect the flame against drafts. A pair of hurricane glasses over your good candlesticks will give a handsome appearance to any sideboard or buffet.

Rush lights were a cheap form of candle. Nothing more than the common reed found in all New England swamps, the "cat-o-nine-tails," dipped in tallow, grease or similar fat, they had their own peculiar holders.

Tapers were yet another form of candle. A thread-like wick soaked in wax or tallow, they were very long and kept wound on a spool.

Along with candles were a variety of utensils needed. Friction matches were not invented until 1827, and even so did not come into general use until later. The usual method of starting a fire was with the use of tinder. Some tinder boxes are still seen around. These little tin boxes were filled with charred linen cloth or some substance which would catch fire easily called tinder, also flint, a piece of iron, and a candle stub. A bit of rough flint with a sharp edge was struck sharply against the piece of iron, causing sparks to fall into the box igniting the tinder. A sulfur-tipped splinter of wood was sometimes used to light the candle stub once the fire was made. The process took some practice to master, even then often taking considerable time compared to modern matches.

With old candles, the wick was not entirely consumed and it was necessary to clip off the charred end of the wick more or less frequently as otherwise it dimmed the flame and made it smoky. A candle snuffer was used; this is a scissor-like instrument for trimming the burnt wick end, which was called "snuff." It was not uncommon to unintentionally put out the candle when snuffing it.

Similar to snuffers in appearance are the "douters" or outquenchers, which were used to extinguish candle flames. In place of the cutting blades and box of the snuffers, these had two disks between which the burning wick was nipped. The name is derived from the practice of instructing servants to "dout the candles," meaning to "do out" the candles. Douters were superseded by the conical extinguishers.

Extinguishers are little, cone-shaped caps which were used to put out candles.

About 1840 came the invention of the non-guttering candlewick and thus a fumeless, slow burning candle not requiring periodic snuffing nor trimming of the wick.

Lanterns were made for both candles and oil lamps. Some have glass sides, some are of tin pierced in patterns. The latter are easy to counterfit: acid treatments and burial in moist earth will give creditable appearance of age and rust.

The first recorded lighting by artificial gas was in 1806 by a D. Melville of Newport, Rhode Island, who manufactured gas and illuminated his house and grounds with it at that date. In 1822 the city of Boston was lighted by gas, but it was not until the decade of 1840-1850 that it came into general use. (It is interesting to note that a revival of this kind of light is taking place at present. The gas companies of many cities advertise gas lights for outdoor lighting.)

So you see, the various forms of lighting were being used even after later developments were introduced. In the more backward parts of the country primitive grease-filled Betty lamps were still in use at the same time more cosmopolitan centers had already progressed to using gas lights. A rural electrification program

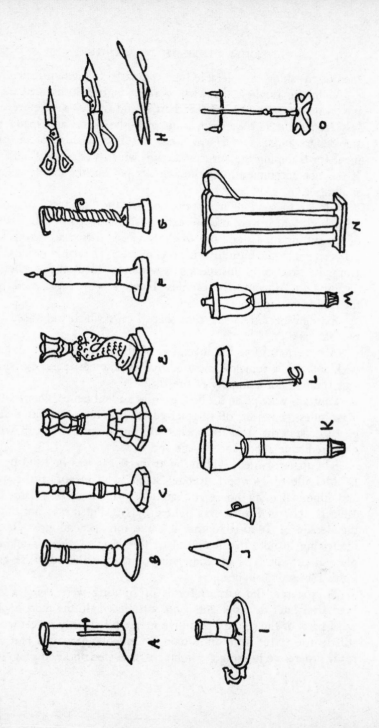

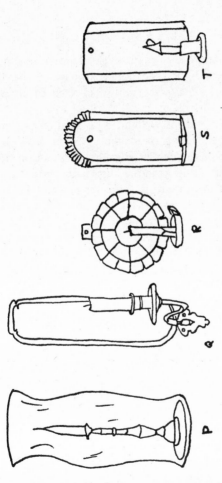

# CANDELIGHT

*A* "hog scraper" candlestick, *B, C, D, E* candle holders, *F* inner-spring candle holder, *G* wrought iron, *H* snuffers, *I* chamber candlestick, *J* extinguishers, *K* inner-spring with holder for shade, made to fit candlestick, *L* shade holder to clip on candle, *M* kerosene lamp made to resemble candle under shade, *N* candle mold, *O* wooden candle stand, *P* hurricane shade, *Q, R, S, T* sconces.

is still in progress in some parts of our country today, including such progressive states as New York.

The range of old lamps and lighting fixtures of the many kinds still around is so great that the collector can choose whatever she prefers, whether dainty or sturdy, decorative or utilitarian.

## GLASS

The myriad shapes and colors of glass, the delicate beauty, the sparkling way it reflects light, and above all else its limitless decorative qualities, make glassware avidly collected in all parts of our country.

Glass can be effectively displayed and is an asset to any room. Put some in your kitchen, living room, dining room, hall, foyer, or parlor. Place it in china cabinets or atop the piano, or on transparent glass shelves in a sunny window. Display it, but use it too.

Due to its fragile nature there is a greater demand for glass than there is supply, which is one reason why so many imitations have been made. There is considerable difficulty in determining the authenticity of glass antiques, and it is only with much comparing against known examples, along with a through knowledge of the subject, that one is able to detect the originals from the later copies.

Glassware is easily reproduced, and many copies have been made of nearly all the more popular patterns and shapes, proving very misleading to the novice collector.

Modern Mexican-made glass is very like the early American and is often mistaken for it. Gift shops display recently made copies of satin glass at a substantially smaller price than their original counterparts, yet remarkably similar.

To distinguish between truly old glass and newer copies is something difficult to learn. Examine the glass in strong daylight rather than artificial light before purchase. There are no infallible rules, no sure signs of age as in furniture; it is more a matter of experience and knowledge combined, which you can develop only through time and patience that enables you to identify the originals.

There were earlier glassworks, but the first successful American glassworks was that of Caspar Wistar, who started his business in 1739 in rural Salem County, New Jersey, near some fine deposits of silica.

There has been little change in the making of glass in the last two hundred or so years. Blown glass is made with the same tools and in the same way now as then. The several processes were done by different men starting with the "gatherer" who took the necessary amount of molten glass from the pots onto the hollow end of a blow pipe (which is a tube about 4 feet long and 1 inch thick.) The "servitor" took over and did the preliminary shaping and then the "gaffer" did the finishing. Various shaped tongs were used to help form the pliable glass into the desired articles. A pontil rod was attached to the end opposite the blow pipe during the process in order to finish the open end of the article, and when the item was finished this pontil rod was removed, making a mark which was usually left, although sometimes ground smooth.

Some early blown glass was enhanced by means of blobs and threads of molten glass applied decoratively to the surface.

After completion, the glass pieces were taken to the annealing oven, in which they were left to be tempered. The annealing process is to remove the brittle quality and make the glass less liable to cracking and breaking. The glass was moved slowly along the annealing ovens through constantly decreasing temperatures until it emerged into room temperature air. This process varied from about twenty-four hours to a week, depending upon the article and its ultimate usage; heavy glass destined for the cutting wheels spent the longest time in the ovens preparing for the friction required to turn it into glittering cut glass.

In modern factories today you will find glass being made this same way.

Fine glass is very hard and rings clearly when struck. This is due to the fact that it is "flint glass," that is, made with sand as a principal ingredient, sand being a form of flint. The distinctive ring is one way it can be told from the less desirable and cheaper lime-glass. This is not, however, any criterion of age; for all good flint glass rings whether made years ago or just last week.

Only blown glass was produced until about 1827 when the mold machine was invented. At first the mold still required the use of the blowpipe and kept its pontil mark. This is called mold-blown glass. Later, stamping machines were used which tamped the molten glass into the mold, leaving no pontil mark.

The molding machines made it possible to produce glass much more cheaply. Many patterns of pressed glass appeared including the much sought Lacey glass.

Lacey glass was a product of the Boston and Sandwich Glass Company operating between 1825 and 1888. Lacey glass obtained its name because of its delicate patterns so suggestive of lace. Early Sandwich glass is noted for its peculiar silvery brilliance.

There are so many kinds and patterns made that the collector, whatever her preference, has a wide choice. You may prefer matching patterns, or you may wish to assemble as many different patterns as possible of the same item.

Among the items sought are cup plates. The small plates were used as a resting plate for a cup while the coffee was being drunk from the saucer. (If you have ever witnessed anyone drinking from a saucer, you will realize why this awkward fashion lasted such a short time—thank heavens—from approximately 1820 to 1850.) These little plates are a prime attraction to many collectors, their small-scale designs being found in some eight hundred patterns, which include conventional sunbursts, hearts, arabesques, geometric designs, and also patriotic motifs of eagles, ships and portraits of important persons of the period. Their small size also allows for many attractive ways to display a collection of cup plates.

Pattern glass consists of the mass-produced pressed glass made in all the forms commonly used in the house. This was the first time the housewife could obtain a complete set of glassware inexpensively, and there were numerous patterns to choose from: some plain, some elaborate in design, some made to resemble the more expensive cut glass—something to suit any taste. Drinking glasses, compotes, bowls, plates, salts, pitchers, pickle jars, celery vases and other items were made in quantity by numerous factories. The most popular patterns today include such well-known titles as: bellflower, daisy and button, horn of plenty, thousand eye, rose in snow, three faces, and westward ho. While searching through some old periodicals in research for this book, the author found one advertisement dated 1886, showing the same cake stand for twenty-five cents that had recently been purchased in a local antique shop for more than five times that amount. Incidents like this make one wonder what the manufacturer would have thought of the increase in value of his humble wares with the passing of time. (Needless to add, this is one of the fascinating reasons for collecting and perusing old magazines and newspapers.)

Earlier glass in the form of flasks, bottles, goblets, and so forth is no more ardently collected than the later Victorian art glass.

Cameo glass has been around since the 1870's, as has Lutz glass. Nicholas Lutz was with the Boston and Sandwich Glass Company during this time, and is known for his delicate striped glass. Reproductions of Lutz glass are currently being made in Italy.

Enameling or painting on glass was popular during the 1870's and 1880's with several excellent artists decorating the glassware of that period. Mary Gregory especially is known for her pictures of children.

Amberina, the glass delicately shading from pale amber color to ruby, was first made by the New England Glass Company in 1883. A lead glass, usually blown, it has remained in popularity a long time and similar glass is still being made today.

Peachblow dates from 1886 and was made by several factories. The name was derived from the Chinese porcelain of that name. Cambridge peachblow glass is found in shades from a cream white to violet red, while the Mt. Washington peachblow ranges from a bluish white to a blush pink. Colorful as it was, peachblow was not a success commercially, therefore little was made and not too much is available today.

Varicolored glass has always appealed to the buying public and was much produced. Spangled glass, a cased glass with spangles or flakes of mica in the inner layer which reflect and sparkle through the colored outer layer, and spattered glass, were popular during the 1880's, as was agata glass. Agata, produced only by the New England Glass Company in 1886, resembled peachblow with a spattered mottling on a glossy finish.

Another varicolored glass is Burmese, which is salmon pink shading to lemon yellow, dating from 1885.

Satin glass and mother-of-pearl satin glass were first made during the 1880's. A treat to the hand as well as to the eye, the beauty of satin glass is enhanced by a satiny finish from which it gets its name. All antique glass may be pretty to look at, and your satin glass will be attractive on display too, but unlike other glass satin glass must be handled and used in order to obtain its full benefits. This kind of glass lends itself particularly well to floral arrangements—a point to keep in mind when shopping for glassware.

The name Tiffany is as familiar to collectors of old glass as it is to those who fancy jewelry. An innovation by Louis C. Tiffany was called Favrile glass and enjoyed an intensive production from 1893 to about 1910. Favrile is known for its iridescent quality and its brilliant deeply toned colors. These articles are marked with the Tiffany name or initials and some bear a number with letters.

Other iridescent glass considered by many as being just as fine as Tiffany's was introduced in 1904 by an Englishman, Fredrick Carder, who was associated with the Steuben Glass Works of Corning, New York (now a part of Corning Glass Company.) Named Aurene, it was made until 1933.

Quezal glass was made from 1917 to 1918 at Quezal Art Glass and Decorating Company in Brooklyn, New York, and was similar to Favrile and Aurene. These are often confused with the glass actually made by Tiffany.

Still other iridescent glass was made by numerous companies in tremendous quantities from 1910 to the late 1920's. Avidly collected from its inception, iridescent glass is found today only in limited amounts.

Cranberry glass had an humble beginning, sold cheaply through mail-order houses and variety stores. The Montgomery Ward catalog of 1895 showed much cranberry glass. The soft color of this glass still pleases us today.

Millefiore glass obtained its name from the Italian word meaning "thousand flowers." Rods of glass of different colors were arranged in bundles, which were then formed into one solid mass. When cut crosswise it showed a delightful pattern resembling a bouquet of tiny flowers. Used for paperweights, it was often set into a ball of plain glass, When blown, the millefiore pattern made most attractive objects such as vases.

Overlay or cased glass is so called because it is made by encasing the glass article within a thin layer or coating of another color glass, or sometimes several layers of different colors over the base. This then is decorated by cutting a design through the outer layer or layers to reveal the glass beneath. This technique had been made earlier in Bohemia and so this type of glass is sometimes referred to as Bohemian glass even though not made there. The overlay is not always cut into patterns; sometimes it is left plain, thus showing a different color glass on the interior than exterior. This was often the case with oil lamp shades which are, indeed, lovely when lit up at night.

Witch balls are blown glass balls with various forms of decoration. They were made in many sizes and colors. It is said that they were made to hang on a cord suspended from the ceiling, and were supposed to repel witches in the mid-Victorian times or later. They have one useful purpose though; they can be used in the necks of vases or jars to keep the dust out. Whether they actually do repel witches is yet to be proved; but they are colorful.

Most cut glass is very heavy and cumbersome. There is a lot of cut glass which does not date back very far, and you should take care in purchasing so you do not buy the late glass mistaking it for the old. Some pressed glass made in imitation of the more expensive cut variety is confusing to the novice collector. If you will

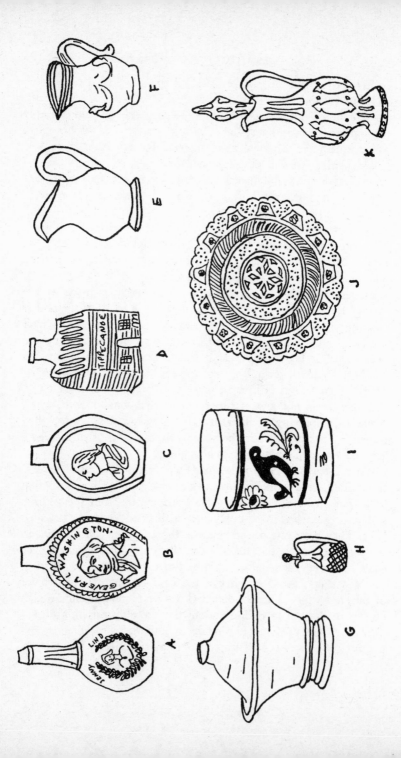

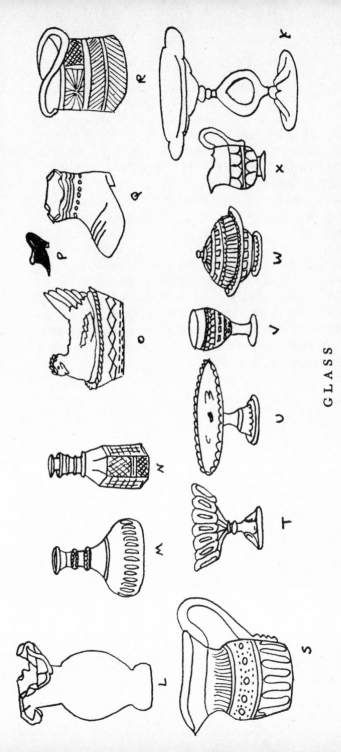

# GLASS

*A, B, C, D* historic flasks, *E, F* blown glass pitchers, *G* blown sugar bowl, *H* pressed glass cruet, *I* enameled glass, *J* lacy glass plate, *K* overlay pitcher, *L* satin glass vase, *M, N* decanters, *O, P, Q* novelties, *R, S* mold blown hat and pitcher, *T, U, V, W, X* pressed glass, *Y* Tiffany dish.

run your fingers over the outside cut-pattern portion of the article, you will soon be able to feel the sharper difference between it and pressed-cut copies. Another tell-tale sign is in the exactness of the pattern itself: since no human hand is as accurate as a machine, there will be places where parts of the pattern are a little off center or just a tiny bit crooked. Buy whichever you like, but at least know the difference and do not pay the higher cut glass price for the less expensive pressed-cut variety out of ignorance. If you entertain a great deal and need large pieces, the pressed copies may very well be a better buy for you since accidental breakage will not be so costly. With the difference saved (and you should actually put aside the difference or there will be no savings) you can purchase finer pieces of the sort used in less hazardous ways.

Old glass is often cloudy in appearance. If this does not respond to washing in hot soapsuds there are other methods that may bring back the original appearance. First try a strong alkaline solution made of soda left standing in the container (it is usually vases and bottles so afflicted) for a week. If no apparent change after washing this out with soap and warm water, then fill the article with vinegar and repeat the process. Sometimes a strong hot soap solution in water and several spoonfuls of small steel (not lead because lead is too soft) shot. Shake the container repeatedly so that the steel shot will come into contact with every part of the stained surface.

If the glass is for display rather than for use, the frosted appearance may be rendered almost clear by the application of ordinary mineral oil or Canada balsam which is applied by the use of cotton batting on the end of a bent wire. This improvement will last longer if the bottle or flask is tightly sealed after the application.

Some glass will not respond to any method and is referred to as "sick glass." If the glass does not respond favorably to any of these methods then it is too sick to cure and must be discarded.

## CHINA

Whether your collection of china is extensive or just a small representation of the various types, you will do well to carefully examine every specimen before purchase.

The novice collector is urged to view, and if possible handle, as many known examples as she can. By carefully inspecting good specimens you soon increase your book knowledge to a practical degree and therefore become more aware of the differences involved between good and just fair specimens.

The popular examples of the many kinds of ceramic wares are frequently copied and there are several ingenious ways by which to artificially create the appearance of age. One of these unscrupulous methods is to allow the piece to bake until the glaze crackles slightly, then to rub with coffee grounds to darken the crackles resembling age. Another way consists of carefully produced nicks and chips to provide a red herring pointing away from its being an imitation. On an unglazed base of a jug many apparent years of usage may be duplicated by the use of a wet grindstone followed by a vigorous rub upon a muddy slate.

China is judged by its scarcity, the quality of its paste, modeling, shape, color and the special characteristics of the factory which produced it. There are so many factors involved that to do justice to the subject would require the length of a book; therefore just the highlights and the types you are likely to find in the average antique shop are touched upon here.

China is often designated by the name of the factory where it was made, such as Dresden, Doulton, Wedgwood, Lambeth, Limoges, Chelsea, Bow, Worcester and so forth.

Porcelain is divided into two general groups: soft-paste and hard-paste. This is due to the differences in the composition of the clay that produces these two with their different characteristics. Advanced collectors are able to perceive these differences, but most of us cannot.

Hard-paste is, as the name implies, harder than the soft-paste. It cannot be easily scratched, is colder to the touch, resists fire and acids, and has a clear ring when struck. The decorative colors seem to stay on the surface. The glazes used on hard-paste porcelain are closely related to the materials of the paste itself and the two are fired at one time, thus they become so fused that along a broken edge you can hardly tell where one ends and the other begins. This is in contrast to most other wares, in which along a broken edge the glaze is clearly visible as a separate coating. (It is not advised, however, to break the item just to determine this fact.) All colors except gold are usually applied before glazing, becoming "under-glaze" coloring.

Soft-paste porcelain differs from hard-paste in that it can be scratched more easily, is warmer to the touch, and the colors of the decoration produce a softer appearance as if they had sunk into the body instead of remaining on the surface. It is not as durable as hard-paste, cracking from contact with hot liquids.

That these differences exist there is no doubt, but the fact remains that few people can accurately tell hard-paste from soft-paste since they look so much alike.

Porcelain is fired at the highest heat of any pottery.

Oriental porcelain, stoneware, ironstone, and most modern china is of the hard-paste variety.

Around 1800 bone ash and other materials were added to the porcelain mixture creating "bone china," which is considered to be midway between hard- and soft-paste porcelains.

Earthenware is of soft body, fired at low heats and generally is opaque and lighter than porcelain. Most household crockery is made of earthenware.

Pottery is a term which includes both the hard, non-porous stoneware and the softer, porous earthenware. It is opaque in contrast to porcelain which is translucent; the simplest way to tell one from another is to hold them up to a strong light. Under this category are included agate wares, marbled wares, delft, stoneware, and the quaint slipware and sgraffiato.

Faïence is a term applied to every kind of glazed earthenware except porcelain. The word is actually French and refers to their enameled wares more particularly.

A glaze is a coating of one of several substances applied to the ware giving it a shiny, glazed surface. One type is the salt glaze, which is produced by throwing a handful of common salt into the heated kiln where the salt vaporizes then settles upon the articles in minute droplets forming a thin, transparent covering. Some forms of glaze are in liquid form and the articles are dipped before firing.

Painted and printed decorations can be done before firing, this being the under-glaze, or after the glaze has been applied, in which case it needs another firing at a lesser heat to fix the colors; this process is known as over-glaze. In either case the colors are of mineral composition, being metallic compounds.

Crazing is the name given the accidental allover cracks that happen because of some defect in the firing or occasionally by removing the china before it has sufficiently cooled.

The decorative possibilities were noted and used purposely by the Chinese who even rubbed coloring matter, usually red, into the cracks to make them more outstanding. Crackle can be produced by coating the article with a glaze that is less sensitive to the heat and expansion than the body of the ware, thus crackling to form a decorative finish.

Another form of decoration is known as slip ware. This consists of a thin clay and water mixture which is painted on, or dropped on in decorative designs from a cup. Sometimes the whole piece was dipped into light-colored slip and then a design was scratched through, exposing the darker clay body, in which case it is known as sgraffiato. These two forms were favored by the Pennsylvania Dutch settlers and were among the first decorated pottery made in our country. They were especially popular in the forms of household wares.

Thin, sliplike decoration applied one layer on top of another until the desired strength is built up is known as *pâte-sur-pâte*.

Still another form of decorating is that of transfer-printing. One of the most favored methods for decorating ceramic wares, it was used extensively. The process was done by the use of an engraved plate; the picture was taken from an engraving onto thin paper which was then pressed upon the surface of the piece while the ink was still wet. When the paper was removed the transfer design remained.

Another method for printing on glazed pottery, which is similar to transfer-printing, is known as bat printing. The design was engraved upon a copper plate which was then given a coat of linseed oil. "Bats" of glue or gelatin were used to take the impression which was then placed upon the pottery, leaving the design which was dusted with the desired color. Firing completed the process. It is similar to transfer-printing in method, but bat printing is on the surface of the glaze, providing a distinguishing characteristic.

Spatter ware is a fairly heavy earthenware with characteristic decoration of color applied with a sponge or spattered on to give a stippled effect. In the center there is generally a clear spot where a design is placed. Often done in bright colors with typical Pennsylvania Dutch motifs, this ware is quaint. Sometimes this is called sponge ware.

Basalt ware is a solid black stoneware with an unglazed surface. It is a striking addition to any collection.

Agate ware resembles the veinings of agate and other natural stones. What is called agate is made by one of two methods: either surface splashes and graining are applied to the surface of a plain body, or layers of different colored clays are twisted together and then cut crosswise with a thin wire. The latter method is considered better.

Porcelain or pottery with shaded or splashed color to the glaze, producing decorative effects, is known as *flambé*.

When the coloring is such that the appearance of tortoise shell is obtained through the use of a sponge and suitable coloring matter, then it is called tortoise-shell ware.

Rockingham ware is made from naturally light colored clay covered with a mottled lead glaze in shades of brown and buff. This earthenware is seen in hound-handled and apostle pitchers as well as in household forms and molds.

Stoneware is composed of a plastic clay with large percentages of silica. It becomes close and hard after firing, into a partly-vitrified opaque pottery, usually with a salt glaze. Stoneware has some characteristics of porcelain, but it is actually earthenware.

Ironstone china is a heavy, durable ware made of earthenware. It was patented in 1813 but reached its greatest popularity from 1820 to late in the century. Ironstone was one of the most important branches of china manufacture. The two most common types are plain white pieces with molded knobs in the shapes of fruit or flowers, and the sepia-printed garden or pastoral scenes showing a Chinese influence. The body contains a large proportion of flint and slag of ironstone from whence this ware receives its name. Inexpensive at the time of manufacture, ironstone china proved very popular from the first.

The Wedgwood factory produced much fine ware of many sorts, but its jasper ware was the one that brought it most fame. To some people the two names are almost synonymous, but this is an erroneous notion.

Jasper ware is a fine, unglazed bisque in various soft colors with white bas-relief designs and figures. Jasper ware was made in several colors, the most popular of which is called "Wedgwood blue." It was made in many forms: vases, medallions, plaques, teapots, and others. Produced as early as 1777, it has been made continually up to and including today.

Parian ware is a hard-paste, unglazed porcelain which resembles marble. It is easily recognized by its granular surface. Parian was molded, the liquid slip being either poured into the mold or pressed in by hand. The interiors of pitchers and vases were often glazed while the pitted exterior remained unglazed. Parian was made in all white or in color, often with white patterns on a colored ground. It was favored for figures and busts.

Delftware is a softer ware of pottery which was dipped in opaque white tin-enamel slip then decorated, with blue being the usual color. This type of ware was first made in Delft, Holland, from which it takes its name.

Creamware is a lead-glazed earthenware, light in weight, creamy both in color and texture. The term is applied to all light-colored English earthenware from 1750 to the present.

Earthenware in naturalistic shapes and decorated with glazes in various colors is majolica. Shapes are often fanciful, such as cauliflower or seaweed and shell. Tin-enameled ware decorated with metallic lustres was made in Majorca off the coast of Spain, and is referred to by the same name although it is a different ware.

Figures were made in several wares. The decorative figures found range from just a few inches tall to nearly thirty inches. The finest figures were made by an intricate process in which all parts were fashioned in separate molds and then assembled. The subjects varied and the figures were made both in porcelain and pottery. Bisque figures are so called from the word "bisque" which is French for biscuit, the term which refers to porcelain or earthenware that has been fired but not glazed.

Staffordshire figures are of soft-paste porcelain and were made in England. Historical and pastoral figures, as well as animals, were made in pairs to be used as mantel ornaments. Among the figures some prominent Americans were portrayed, including Abraham Lincoln and Benjamin Franklin. Little houses or cottages with vines and flowers were also made, as was transfer-printed china which often had American historical views.

Made in England also were Liverpool jugs. These were pitchers or jugs with transfer designs. The decorations were often of American subject matter, with ships and celebrated men of the times most represented.

Another English ware which was made especially to appeal to American trade is Gaudy Dutch. This china was aimed at the Pennsylvania Dutch market and is characterized by bold designs and bright colors. Flowers, leaves, and line borders were the most usual patterns. Designs on this china were handpainted with a free-hand stroke over the glaze.

Similar to Gaudy Dutch is Gaudy Welsh. In this ware the weight and texture of the china are more related to spatterware and the shapes are cruder and heavier. The coloring is bold and bright, but crude. Tulips were often represented in the designs.

Toby jugs are those quaint, and often grotesque, little jugs formed in the likeness of a man whose large hat forms the spout.

The willow pattern is the most popular pattern ever applied to pottery; it depicts the sad story of an old Chinese legend.

The willow pattern in its present form was originated in 1780 by an Englishman, Thomas Turner of Caughley Pottery Works. Subsequently there have been more than two hundred makers of this famous design. The pattern tells the legend of a beautiful Chinese girl, named Koon-Shee, and her mandarin father. They lived in the large pagoda seen under the apple tree. The little bridge, the willow tree, and the fence are all integral parts of the story. It seems that the mandarin had promised his daughter as the bride of a wealthy, but old, merchant. The daughter, however, had other ideas because she was in love with Chang, her father's secretary, and she ran away with him. The father pursued the lovers and all three can be seen on the little bridge: the first figure that of the girl carrying a distaff, the emblem of virginity, then Chang carrying a box containing jewels, and following him is the furious mandarin carrying a whip and black thoughts. Eventually, goes the legend, he did overtake them and ordered both young people put to death. Before his terrible order could be carried out, sympathetic gods transformed the runaway lovers into turtledoves, which are seen flying overhead in the pattern.

The willow pattern differs only slightly by different potters, mostly in the number of apples upon the tree and in the fence design. The main distinguishing characteristic is to be found in the borders around the edge of the plates. This, in addition to the other small variations from one potter to another, help determine the maker. The value of willow pattern depends upon the scarcity of the pieces as produced by the particular maker as well as the condition of the article itself.

Lustre ware is another extremely popular item with collectors. The lustrous finish applied to the potters humble ware is a very old method of decoration. It is believed to have been first made by the Moors in Spain in the seventh century. The lustrous effect is obtained by applying a thin coating of certain metallic oxides which differ with the color produced. Colors include pink, purple, copper and silver. These were made in allover plain finishes and in decorative bands and designs. Early silver lustre was an imitation of silver, made in similar designs and lustred both inside and out. Later only the outside was lustred.

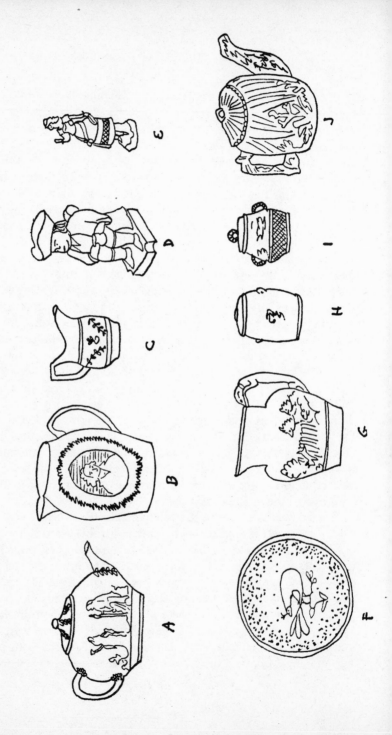

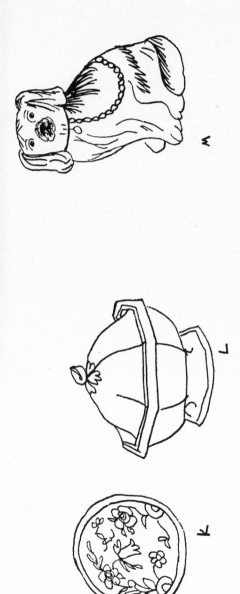

## C H I N A

A jasper ware teapot, *B* Liverpool jug, *C* luster pitcher, *D* Toby jug, *E* bisque figure, *F* spatter ware plate, *G* hounds head pitcher, *H* stoneware, *I, J* Majolica, *K* Gaudy Dutch plate, *L* ironstone tureen, *M* Staffordshire "Comforter" mantel dog.

Resist lustre is another form of lustre ware in which the background of the article appears in the lustre and the design shows in white or colored pottery. This was accomplished by painting the desired pattern with a material which resists the effects of the lustre coating. Then the whole item was dipped into the metallic solution so that all but the covered design became lustred. After drying, the surfaces were washed, removing the resist and leaving the pattern silhouetted against a lustred ground. Then the piece was fired and became resist lustre ware.

Lustre ware is still being made today and so the collector must beware, or she is very likely to be fooled by a later piece.

## ENAMEL

Enamels are metals or porcelain which are covered with color and then fired. The coloring matter consisted of easily fusible glass of the desired colors which are opaque or semi-transparent according to the mixtures of metallic oxides used.

Battersea enamels of England are a good example of this ware. These are enamel upon a thin copper base, which was then decorated by hand painting or transfer-printing.

Cloisonné is another enamel, the design for which was outlined by wires soldered to the surface of the body. The hollow spaces were then filled with the enamel paste, rubbed down smooth, and heated until they ran smoothly over the surface to which they adhered by fusion with the metal.

## PEWTER

The gray, silvery sheen of pewter has been a delight to the eyes of countless generation of collectors. It was used for ecclesiastical purposes even before it became a part of the household to begin its long career meeting domestic requirements.

One of the oldest composite metals known, the first recorded mention of pewter as table ware was in the year 1274, at the coronation banquet of Edward I of England, who owned three hundred pieces at that time.

Pewter has been made more or less steadily from very early times until present; the most active period of the ancient craft was from about 1700 to 1850. As recently as 1907 the firm of Reed & Barton Silversmiths advertised pewter in the *Ladies' Home Journal* with the statements that, "The present day is witnessing a remarkable revival in the use of pewterware. Antiquated tea sets, kettles, candlesticks, tankards, etc. . . ." Much pewter of this vintage is today being passed off as much older.

The quality of pewter varies considerably. The finest quality consisted of 112 parts of tin to 26 parts of copper; a medium grade was made up of 100 parts of tin to 17 parts of antimony; and the cheapest and poorest quality, which was also known as black metal, was simply 60 parts of tin to 40 parts of lead. Good pewter can be recognized by its weight, color and feel.

A soft metal with low melting point, pewter can be easily worked. It can be cast in molds, spun, or rolled into sheets and then hammered into the desired shapes.

When domestic articles became too battered and misshapen from use, they were not repaired, but instead were melted down and recast. Spoons particularly, received hard wear and were often recast, which is why we find so many molds for pewter spoons handed down through the years.

Some, but not all, pewter will be found with a touch-mark. This is like the hallmark on silver to distinguish the maker.

Among the items you will find made of pewter are plates, candlesticks, oil lamps, teapots, spoons, bowls, basins, tankards, mugs, porringers, inkwells, pitchers and flagons. The older the piece the more likely it is to be simple in form. The more elaborate specimens were a little later.

Pewter darkens and dulls, but it is not difficult to clean. Ordinary kitchen scouring powder moistened with a little kerosene will clean most darkened ware, but if the tarnish is very bad you might try either fine steel wool or fine emery cloth, being careful to use them sparingly so as not to cut too deeply into the soft metal. For regular cleaning, either silver polish or light oil rubbed on with a soft cloth will be sufficient. Whatever cleaning methods

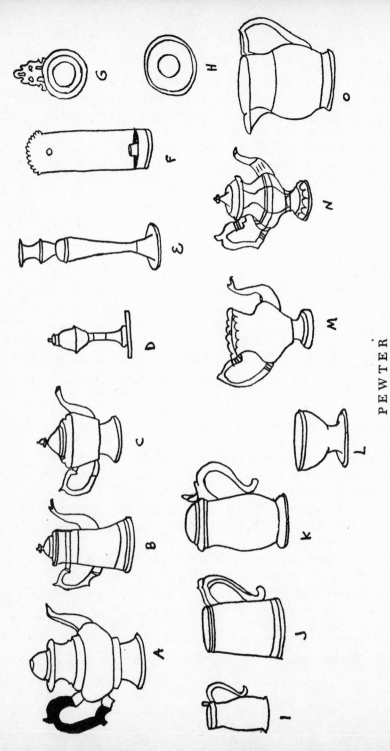

PEWTER

*A, B, C* pewter teapots, *D* whale-oil lamp, *E* candlestick, *F* sconce, *G* porringer, *H* plate, *I, J, K* tankards, *L* salt, *M, N, O* britannia ware teapots and pitcher.

you use, be sure to wash thoroughly with soap and water afterwards.

## BRITANNIA

After 1820, britannia metal began to displace pewter in popularity. Britannia, actually a high grade pewter, was occasionally called white metal and was closer in appearance to silver than to pewter. Its composition varied a little, but usually was 85 per cent tin, 10 per cent antimony, 3 per cent zinc and 1 per cent copper. Bismuth was often added.

Britannia ware was made in designs similar both to pewter and silver, and has been found in all the same forms as solid silver of the same period. Teapots appeared in larger sizes than previously, due to the fact that tea was so much more plentiful. The tea set, consisting of teapot, creamer and sugar bowl all of matching designs, were made to be used together. Candlesticks in britannia are numerous.

Many handsome examples of britannia ware were made, although today the earlier pewter is more highly treasured.

## SILVER

Silver, always a symbol of wealth, was at one time actually that. Having no banks, the people with extra coins took them to a silversmith to be turned into useful household articles. Thus, the money of their day brought not only wealth but utility and beauty into the home. From a silver coin to a spoon was a common transposition.

Silver followed the changes in styles and can be found in many pleasing shapes and forms. Early American silver reflects the lives and times which produced it. Its simplicity of line and graceful forms exhibit a delightful charm.

Surface decoration was in good taste as well as superb workmanship. In making hollow ware the metal was rolled into sheets and beaten with a mallet into the desired shape. The surface decoration, if any, was then added to the article. Ornamentation took several forms: engraving, which consisted of marking with a sharp tool that removed a portion of the surface; chasing, done with tools without a cutting edge by displacing the metal through pressure; *repoussé*, a relief decoration accomplished by hammering instead of by slow pressure, as in chasing; and piercing a pattern.

The word "sterling" began appearing on silver around 1865 to denote silver up to standard. Some silver before that time was of equal quality, but it was not until the term sterling came into use that the buyer was assured of the exact quality purchased. Pure silver is considered 1000 parts fine, while coin silver is 900 parts fine; sterling silver is made up of 925 parts pure silver and 75 parts copper for strength.

## SHEFFIELD

Sheffield plate looked like silver on the surface but actually was a sheet of copper surrounded on both sides with thin sheets of silver. This was the poor man's silverware. Sheffield was made in nearly all the same styles as silver popular at the same time.

The Sheffield that has survived the ravages of time has worn down considerably through constant handling and polishings, often to a point where the copper shows. Once this happens there is nothing that can be done, for it has lost its value and is practically worthless. Some people have worn Sheffield replated by modern means, but of course once this is done it is no longer Sheffield, but just an old article which even lacks patina.

## PLATED SILVER

Electroplating was invented about 1840. It became popular immediately because it brought plated silver within the price range of average people. Previous to that time silver was strictly a luxury item.

The plating did not have to be thick, .001 of an inch was sufficient just as long as it was of uniform thickness all over.

Several bases were used for silver plated wares: nickel silver (an alloy of copper, zinc and nickel), copper, and white metal. Often you will find the letters EPN, EPC, or EPWM on the bottom of plated silver indicating which metal was used for the base.

## BUYING SILVER

Unless Sheffield or plated silver is in EXCELLENT shape it is a poor buy, regardless of the price.

Sterling silver can never be worn away to expose another metal for it is all silver and therefore is a lifetime investment.

If you cannot afford to buy fine old sterling or authenticated coin silver, it might be wiser to purchase sterling reproductions from one of the several firms which have been continuously producing the same good quality over a century or more, than to buy items in which the silver is already worn or wearing off.

In silver, just as in everything else, you should buy the best you can afford, keeping in mind the style, age and condition.

Early silver possesses a soft lustrous color and texture which is unmatched in modern pieces and should *never* be buffed. The patina acquired by the passing of the years through usage and polishings is best cleaned by the use of any good quality silver polish (the author prefers a paste polish) a soft cloth or celonese sponge, along with some good, old-fashioned "elbow grease." *Never* use the quick-cleaning methods involving chemicals, for that destroys the oxidation (the black coloring in the fine depressions of the design) and gives a harsh, tinny color to the silver.

The beautiful appearance of fine silver enhances the room in which it is displayed, and improves any meal, no matter how simple. Owning and using silver is well worth the little effort needed keeping it polished.

# SILVER

A flagon, B, C tankards, D, E, F, G, H teapots, I bowl by Paul Revere 1768, J, K casters, L cream pitcher, M porringer, N, O silver salts, P pierced basket, Q caster set, R candelabrum, S candlestick, T late jar.

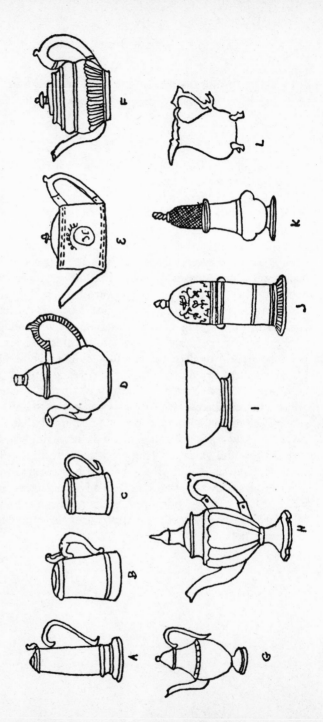

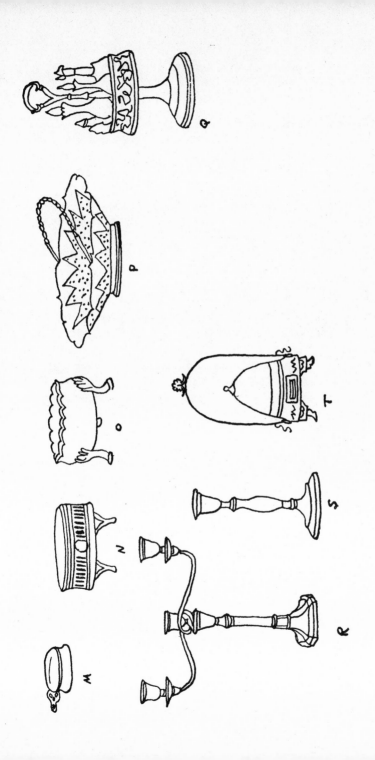

## BRASS AND COPPER

More brass antiques will be found than copper. As brass is an alloy (of copper and zinc) and therefore harder and firmer, it was used more often. Its goldlike color has made it a widespread favorite over many years.

Almost every household article necessary can be found in brass: lamps, candlesticks, trivets, warming pans, andirons, fenders, pots, kettles, teakettles, kitchen tools (skimmers, ladles, etc.), jamb hooks, furniture hardware (handles, escutcheons, knobs, keys, hinges), mortar and pestles, door knockers, inkwells and other desk accessories, mirror knobs, drapery tie backs, wall brackets, ormolu furniture mounts, jardinieres, much Victorian furniture including plant stands, hall racks, and the familiar brass beds.

Cast brass made before 1830 has a pencil thin line extending from top to bottom on both sides, because they were cast in two halfs and then braised together. Andirons of this period, when unscrewed, will show this line on the interior most clearly. After 1830, brass articles were cast in one piece and do not show this line.

Polished brass has a lovely sheen closely resembling gold. It can become tarnished, sometimes to the point where it is actually mistaken for iron, if left long enough. There are several commercial brass polishes on the market; but the easiest way to clean tarnished brass is by the use of ordinary soap-impregnated steel wool pads (such as S.O.S) that you use to clean and shine your pots and pans. You can use water liberally when cleaning brass, then wipe dry with a soft cloth. If the brass is very badly tarnished it can be cleaned by the use of carborundum valve-grinding compound from any auto supply store. Clear lacquer can be used to protect a bed or other large article from frequent polishings, and colorless nail polish can be used for jamb hooks, mirror knobs, and other tiny items.

This pine chest has magnificent hand-made hardware (a huge lock and strap hinges which go completely under and around the chest). Above is a framed sampler. The quilts were made by author.

A charming Victorian bedroom in a modern home. Brass bed and banquet lamp with walnut furniture and a mono-cromatic color scheme. The quilt was made by author.

Simple furniture can be painted and decorated to your needs inexpensively, as shown in this cheerful attic spare room.

This painted wagon seat makes the rose garden even more enjoyable. The sun was too strong to show the decorations, which are Pennsylvania Dutch.

Some early lighting devices, from a pine knot through kerosene lamps.

A legless dough tray made into a dog house, a porringer for water. Block front desk in background.

## TIN

A lightweight, inexpensive metal, tin was used for many items: teapots, plates, platters, trays, boxes, candle molds, lamps, sconces, foot warmers, lanterns, canisters, tea caddies, and so on.

Much tinware was lacquered or painted, producing the colorful articles known as Japan ware and tole ware.

Before buying painted tin, inspect it to see whether the decorations are of old lacquer which will appear slightly worn, the colors softened by age, and possibly crazed; or whether the paint job is a new one, possibly hiding some far-from-old tinware.

## IRON

There is a distinction between cast iron and wrought iron that is easily discerned, yet few people seem to know the difference. The very titles are descriptive of the processes which produce them: cast iron is iron which has been cast into a mold, and wrought iron has been made by various hand processes. There is, however, still a further distinction. Wrought iron can be obtained in thin bars then bent and twisted into elaborate designs (the Spanish made beautiful gates like this, and a modern example is the common porch railing), or it can be forged from a bar of iron, worked via hammer and anvil until it has been coaxed into the desired form—this is true hand-wrought iron and is the most highly prized. Unless iron is hand forged it cannot be called "hand wrought" even though it is wrought iron. It would be just as sensible to call all twisted iron hand wrought as it would be to call all dresses handmade just because someone had to cut the pattern and pin the fittings by hand, doing only the actual sewing on the machine; or as one television comedian recently stated, "All my clothes are hand tailored—that means my tailor has hands."

Some time ago while buying used lumber to build a tool shed, the author spied a handmade nail on the ground. The man in charge of the yard said they had razed several very old houses, didn't want the old nails, and to "take as many as you want." I felt terribly foolish picking up nails amid the rubble (not to mention the danger, for it was summer and I was wearing sandals), but it was worth while. Now those same nails, clean but still crooked, support a collection of hand-wrought trivets above the stove where they are convenient for the constant use they receive.

Iron antiques are to be found making up fireplace equipment, andirons, cranes, trammels, pot hooks, toasters, pots, griddles, cauldrons, as well as sad irons, foot scrapers, candlesticks, candlestands, lamps, weather vanes, snuffers, wick-trimmers, extinguishers, curling irons, wall brackets of many kinds, and much early hardware.

Rust is no deterrent to acquiring antiques made of iron. It is easy to clean rust from old iron: rubbing with steel wool and kerosene will take off most rust; stubborn spots may have to be soaked in the kerosene for an hour first, then wiped dry and oil applied. Allow the oil to soak in for a few days, then wipe off whatever remains. With utensils that you wish to use for cooking, wash well with soap and water after the kerosene-steel-wool treatment, dry carefully, and coat lightly with salad oil. Iron must be dried thoroughly after each washing or else it will rust again.

## CLOCKS

The first methods of telling time consisted only of watching the sun and the stars in their regularly spaced journeys across the heavens.

By observing the lengthening and diminishing shadows of the trees the idea of the sundial was derived.

Hourglasses, or sand glasses, the same as you use today to time soft boiled eggs, were used in a larger size very early in history. They are mentioned as early as 1550 B.C.

Along with hourglasses, water clocks were the first mechanical time-telling devices. The water clock, which was introduced into Greece by Plato, was a vessel with a hole through which the water escaped; the level of the remaining water denoted the time. The ancient Greeks adjusted their water clocks to denote the amount of remaining daylight, whatever the season. This seems to be the forerunner to our annoying daylight saving time.

Candles were another early method for telling time. The candle was marked off in inches which burned at the rate of twenty minutes per inch, thus giving a fairly accurate measure.

By combining these last two methods for telling time, the time lamp was invented. The pewter lamp, similar to the Betty lamp in shape and design, differed in that it had a glass font on top to hold the oil. This oil font is marked with Roman numerals to denote the hours, so that the gradual lowering of the oil as the lamp burned registered the time. One was found a few years ago in a small antique shop. It was in excellent condition, but the glass font was missing. Upon inquiring the price, the customer was informed, "You can have that old ashtray for two dollars."

The first modern clock was invented in the thirteenth century. It had but one hand and a balance or fly-wheel escapement. In the middle of the seventeenth century, the minute hand was added along with the pendulum.

A little later the spiral spring clock was made, as was the one run by weights. Clocks driven by the coiled spring method were more expensive and more complicated than those driven by falling weights, because when only the cords broke they were easily replaced, while a broken spring was a major repair job.

Contrary to logical thinking, metal works in clocks are older than wood. The wooden works were much cheaper to make than brass and were manufactured from the 1790's to around 1835. Metal-work clocks also were made during the same time.

The long pendulum swinging below the clock on the wall gave to it the name of "Wag-on-the-wall" clock.

By enclosing this whole in a standing case the grandfather clock came into being. About 1700 this distinguished type of tall clock was developed with a heavy cornice and a flat top. By 1725 cabinetmakers added the hood with its graceful arched top. The grandfather clock was now a lovely piece of furniture, harmonious with the Chippendale furniture fashionable at that time.

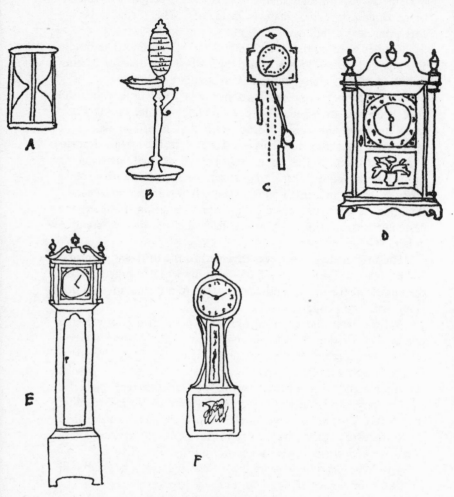

## TIMEPIECES

*A* hourglass, *B* pewter time lamp, *C* wag-on-the-wall clock, *D* pillar and scroll clock, *E* grandfather's clock, *F* Banjo clock.

Smaller clocks of the same general appearance as the grandfather clocks are known, logically, as grandmother clocks.

The cases of clockworks, being furniture, vary with the different styles. These cases were sometimes made by the clockmaker, but more often by a cabinetmaker. Some are very elaborate. J. Goddard is known to have made block front clocks circa 1765.

An "improved timepiece" was invented in 1801 by Simon Willard and is now called the banjo clock. The works of this banjo-shaped clock were of brass and had great accuracy. Made to hang on the wall with a small bracket to help support it, this popular clock was imitated by other makers and the pattern became well known.

The "pillar and scroll" clock first made by Eli Terry in 1814 was one of the first, if not the very first, articles to be made by quantity production and in the popular-priced field. A pleasingly shaped mantel clock, the pillar and scroll was made both with wood and brass works, and ran thirty hours. They were produced for twenty-five years or more and were exported to foreign countries in large numbers.

The steeple clock of the mid-nineteenth century was another popular mantel clock. It takes its name from the steeplelike appearance of its case.

## MIRRORS

Considered as furniture, mirrors were made in many styles and sizes from small courting glasses to full length cheval glasses.

Early looking-glasses had wide bevels around the edge following the frame. This was very slight but can be felt by rubbing the fingers gently over the glass. In contrast, the modern bevel is sharp and distinct.

Shaving mirrors are those nice little mirrors set on a frame above several small drawers. They were made in many different styles, and give a decorative touch to any room as well as being a handy aid to last-minute primping.

Cheval glasses are large mirrors on standing frames. For the house without a full length mirror, one of these is the answer to straight seams and even hems. These too, were made in several styles.

Consider the decorative aspects of mirrors and use them to fullest advantage in your house. Place the mirror where its reflection will repeat a pleasant setting or create a sense of space to a small area. Strategically placed mirrors can improve your home decor greatly.

## MINIATURES

These charming little articles are to be found in almost every variety of furniture. There is considerable difference of opinion as to the original purposes of miniature furniture. Some sources contend that they were made as children's toys for doll furniture, while others just as vehemently state that they were samples of a convenient size for salesmen to carry around in order to sell the full-size models. Whatever the first reasons for making miniature furniture, they are lovely little articles with a multitude of uses today.

Miniature chests of drawers are especially desirable for their tiny storage areas in such a decorative setting. Ideal for gloves and scarves, as a jewelry box, for handkerchiefs, stockings, or any small items which must be kept handy. One can be used as a sewing box, its little drawers holding scissors, needles, threads, odd buttons, hooks and eyes, pin cushion and tape measure. For the woman who sews it might also keep her patterns filed away neatly.

## JEWELRY

Many antique shops carry jewelry which is not nearly as old as their furniture, yet still is considered in the realm of the antique.

Jewelry is a personal item, and its purchase must necessarily entail more than intrinsic value. Here, age is less of a criterion for desirability than in other articles. The primary factors to consider are your individual wardrobe and your wallet.

Even the less expensive antique jewelry will prove more

unique than what you could purchase for the same amount of money at a department store. Often an unusual brooch or necklace will be just the thing to set off a plain dress.

Unusual buttons can sometimes be made into earrings with pleasing results.

Stickpins can be turned into other articles of jewelry such as charms for a bracelet, tie tacks, or scatter pins.

When you chance across old jewelry outside of a shop inspect it carefully, for often the old silver or brass used is so tarnished as to be passed by, while all that is needed is a good cleaning in order to produce a nice addition to your collection at a microscopic cost.

## BOOKS

First editions and other rare printings are strictly for the collector of old books. Their scarcity and the consequently high prices put them out of the category of collectable antiques for the casual collector.

There were so many books printed, however, that most of them are inexpensive today. These books often have interesting subject matter which is told in quaint, obsolete styles. Some of the most fascinating of old books consist of the aged cook books with their funny old recipes. "Receipts" that are vague in directions and have impossible measurements. Etiquette of the bygone days was written about in all seriousness, and yet today, books on this subject are most often hilarious. It makes one wonder if our manners and the protocol we observe now will change as much, and if our descendants will find us as humorous as this "Common Breach of Table Etiquette" described so exactly:

It is ill-bred to take soup audibly. Indeed, yes, it is a breach of table etiquette that one should have been taught to avoid in nursery days. The lapse from proprieties is easily avoided if the upper lip touch the liquid and the breath be but slightly inhaled. Although soup should, of course, be taken from the side of the spoon, persons with mustaches have a "special dispensation" if they find that they must take its point into the mouth.

Interesting old maps and illustrations of all kinds are to be found in old books, many of which are suitable for framing. A word of caution here: do *not* cut up any book until you know for sure that it is not a valuable edition.


## PERIODICALS

Old magazines and newspapers offer hours of interesting reading for the antique lover, as well as contain many items of general interest and amusement to anyone who leafs through them.

The daily lives and events of the past are always of interest, but the long forgotten advertisements prove of greatest fascination for two seemingly opposing reasons: the differences from today, and strangely enough, the similarities. Many of the same manufacturers who supply us with commodities at present have been in business for more than fifty years; their early ads seem as familiar as old friends in strange clothing.

How to reduce FAT.
It is purely vegetable and many can easily prepare it at home at little expense. No starving, No sickness. Send 4¢ for a Sample box and full particulars in a plain envelope.

Sound familiar? That advertisement appeared in an 1896 newspaper, along with "Thrilling Tales of Indian Massacres," cures for piles, a "sure cure" for excessive drinking, illustrated ads for corsets, pocket knives, crochet silk, self-threading needles, jewelry, pressed glass, kitchenware, razor blades, linen towels, Bibles, china, an original ad for Lydia E. Pinkham, and of course, the inevitable needlework patterns.

Advertisements can be found for removing superfluous hair, dyeing old dresses, keeping the desired amount of curl to your hair, making money at home, and enlarging your bust. These could have come from the same magazines you read under the dryer at the beauty shop, so similar are they.

The most enjoyable of all periodicals are the women's magazines. Despite the changing world affairs and the passage of three wars, a depression, inflation, recession, unemployment, and sputnicks, women still remain basically unchanged. It is comforting to know that long ago, as today, women had the same problems of hair curling, hose supporters, face powder, dieting, and devices to keep their "waists" and skirts together.

Periodicals accurately reflect the daily living and give a clear picture of life at the time of publishing. Therein lies their charm. Fashions and quoted prices along with such articles as "$1,500 a Year for Young Couple and Maid" which appeared early in the century in the *Ladies' Home Journal* (and by the way, included not only the full-time maid but also a cleaning woman once a week) should prove amusing to Husband. As a housewife, you will appreciate the obsolete patterns, recipes, home made beauty preparations and grooming hints.

An old magazine or two left lying on the coffee table will prove entertaining to all who have access to your living room.

# Accessories to Go With Antiques

EVERY HOUSE NEEDS ACCESSORIES, and the antique collector's home is no exception. Many of these accessories may be antiques themselves or, if not, they should be natural companions to the antiques which provide the furnishings for the house.

The effectiveness of any accessory depends a great deal upon the attractive grouping or arrangement which it helps compose, along with a pleasing background.

No matter what the intrinsic value of an object, its beauty can be dimmed by placing it against an inharmonious background, and increased by the right setting. Color, size, and texture must be taken into consideration, and the accessories arranged pleasingly.

## PICTURES

There are many fine paintings done by obscure artists and even some excellent unsigned paintings which can be had for a reasonable sum.

Framed engravings, such as the famous Currier and Ives prints, provide interesting pictures for the antique collector, as also do paintings on glass.

Subject matter varies from the realistic portraits of someone's ancestors to the quaint, primitive style such as that done by Grandma Moses.

There are many other items which can be framed and hung on the walls for pictures. These include a vast number of small items: needlework pictures, framed documents, such as the quaint Pennsylvania Dutch fractors, early maps and samplers.

## ARTIFACTS AND OTHER ITEMS
## HUNG ON THE WALLS

Other articles to be hung on the wall cover collections of many kinds. Mounting or framing can display collections to their fullest advantage. If it was worth collecting it is worth displaying.

These can be framed or displayed upon brackets, shelves, or hanging whatnots. This group covers collections of buttons, coins, fans, sea shells, arrow heads, porcelain figurines, carved animals, miniature lamps, decorative and memorial spoons, gold toothpicks, trivets, snuff boxes, paper clips, match book covers, or whatever is closest to your heart. There is supposed to be a difference between collecting and accumulating—but just when this occurs no one seems to know.

Be sure to hang these items at eye level so that you can best enjoy them.

In addition to the above articles, such things as stuffed trophies and antlers, muzzle loading rifles, dueling pistols, witch balls, plates, platters, wooden cake molds, dried Indian corn, candle sconces and mirrors are also hung upon the walls.

All these items can be most attractively displayed along with your antique furniture. They are the articles you like to look at, and which at the same time provide the individual touch to your home—the final cherry to the top of the most perfect sundae.

## FIREPLACE ACCESSORIES

If you are fortunate enough to have a fireplace in your house you will need andirons. Choose iron or brass in whichever style will best suit your other furnishings.

Add a crane, pots, kettles, poker, bellows, toaster, bread peel, and all of the early accompaniments if you like, or just andirons, tools and a fender.

A warming pan of brass or copper will enhance the appearance of any fireplace.

Over the mantel you can place a large mirror, an impressive picture, or an old blunderbuss.

## INKWELLS

Whether you use a fountain pen or not, an inkstand will be an attractive addition to any antique desk.

Inkwells have been made in many materials: turned wood, pewter, porcelain, brass and silver. Some are quite elaborate while others are completely utilitarian. The style of your desk will supply the requirements.

## QUILL PENS

Quill pens are still being made for use in Congress. They are a little difficult to get used to after all the years of writing with fountain pens and lately ball point pens, but any of you who are old enough to remember the penmanship exercises in school with their seemingly endless rows of squiggles will know that after a while it is simple. In all events they do look decorative atop the desk along with an antique inkwell. (Incidentally, the little knife called a "pen knife" got its descriptive name from being used to cut a new nib in the feather as it was worn down.)

## CURTAIN TIEBACKS

Drapery tiebacks can be used just as they are; the most interesting ones by far are those made of glass in the form of rosettes. Other suitable items can be used in the same manner.

Some round horse-collar ornaments are decorative enough to be made into pretty tiebacks with no one the wiser.

The degree of formality and the general decor of the room will suggest other articles to you.

## NEEDLEWORK IN GENERAL

There is a certain satisfaction for the woman who does needlework of any kind; it consists of the sweet feeling of accomplishment, as well as the relaxing enjoyment of the actual work.

In this age of mechanization, it is refreshing to enter a home where the woman has taken the time and trouble to create something lovely with her own hands. Unlikely as it seems, it is usually the proud Husband who most appreciates a woman's handiwork.

The charm of yesteryear was in a large way due to the handiwork of the people themselves: from sturdy, handmade furniture to delicate needlework.

## SAMPLERS

Framed samplers adorn many walls. The sampler might be an authentically old one or it can be one you have made yourself. If you make your own, keep in mind that the very old ones were of excellent workmanship with tiny stitches, individual patterns, and usually pious verses. Biblical scenes were often represented, with Adam and Eve one of the most favorite; also flowers and birds were rampant.

Unbleached linen was used for the basis of the embroidery.

## NEEDLEPOINT

Needlepoint, both petit point and gros point, is simple to learn. You can make your own covers for chair seats, footstools or complete chairs (which will require professional upholstering).

## CREWELWORK

Colorful wools embroidered upon unbleached linen provides an interesting departure from the usual needlework done by the modern woman. This will give you a chance to use up those odds and ends of wool left over from needlepoint, knitting, or crocheting.

The "tree of life" patterns were always popular. These depict leaves, buds, flowers and occasionally fruit, all on the same tree. Primitive little animals and large birds or butterflies all out of proportion with the rest of the work were added. Chair seats and curtains of this work are most attractive. You can also use butcher linen for the base since it resembles true linen in appearance closely, but at a much lesser cost; however, it does not wear as well.

## RUGS: HOOKED AND BRAIDED

Both of these types of floor coverings look good with antique furniture. Here you have your choice of old rugs, modern copies, or making them yourself.

The making of a rug is a tremendous undertaking which only the most ambitious will tackle. Small throw rugs, however, are not so arduous a task; and little pads for the seats of wooden chairs, even less.

## QUILTS

Any woman who can sew a neat hem in a dress can make a patchwork quilt. For the woman who sews, this is a goood way to use up the bits of washable material from her scrap basket.

There are frames which resemble oversized embroidery hoops, for quilt making. These can be easily carried about so that the quilt can be worked on at your convenience, and then put out of the way.

There are many delightful old patterns available which will give your bedrooms an air of authenticity in the exact colors you desire. The American-born Duchess of Windsor has lovely harlequin-patterned quilts in her home just outside Paris, shown recently in a national magazine.

Quilts were made with elaborately pieced tops as well as crazy quilt patches; with appliquéd patterns and with the pattern worked out all in the actual quilting. Use a good filling made for that purpose * and color-fast fabrics. When made this way, quilts can be washed in a tumbler type automatic washer and dried in an automatic drier to emerge fluffier and prettier with each washing.

Many women find needlework of any kind relaxing, and quilt-

---

* Note: Stearns and Foster Company, Cincinnati, Ohio, the manufacturer of "Mountain Mist" quilt filling, have directions and patterns available.

making heads the list. During a long evening of television or on a quiet summer's afternoon it cannot be surpassed.

A quilt makes a pretty bedspread, and in addition it doubles as a light-weight blanket. Extra blankets are always useful, and a quilt is light enough to use throughout the summer months, when, in some parts of the country, a wool blanket is unbearable. The author has made many quilts, of old patterns as well as of her own designs, and recommends quilt-making highly.

## EXTERIOR ACCESSORIES

The exterior of your house is what first greets the eye of your visitor, and is the only part seen by the many people who drive past daily.

This facet of your home need not be neglected. It can provide a provocative hint as to the interior, and distinguish you from your neighbors at the same time.

A weather vane for the roof is a good place to start. Then you might add shutter fasteners, a foot scraper, and lastly, a brightly polished door knocker.

If you have a small porch you might add some potted plants in suitable containers, and possibly a little bench or settee.

## DOGS AND CATS

Your dog is a bona fide member of your family and should be included when it comes to antiques, too.

Start with his water dish. Whatever kind of a dish Rover eats his dinner from, it is duly washed and put away until the next meal; but not so his water dish. There it sits, day and night, an eyesore for all to behold. Have you thought of giving him an antique bowl? Not a priceless example of the potters' art, but just a poorer example, a trifle crooked or a little off-color, of whatever kind you collect. Consider it to be on display at floor level instead of in your china cabinet. It will serve admirably for holding fresh water, and be much prettier to look at than the typical dog dish from the pet shop. There are endless sizes and shapes in glass—blown, pressed or cut; and in china—painted china, porcelain or pottery; enough to suit any dog, large or small, and any pocketbook, large or small. In Buffalo there are two little Chihuahuas that share a really elegant footed candy dish of pierced silver with a glass insert—the portion where the plating is worn off would be apparent if at table level but does not show at all on the floor.

Every dog deserves a soft bed of his own. This should be free from drafts and, if possible, raised a little, rather than setting directly on the floor. Often dogs are subject to drafts of which we are not aware. This is especially true of the smaller breeds. A soft washable blanket or old turkish towel on top of Rover's mattress will give him just the right place to scrunch down into (this is what he wants when he turns around in little circles before lying down to sleep) and will be easy to toss into the washing machine for cleanliness.

Many little dogs like the feeling of being sheltered, and will crawl into closets or under furniture for their forty winks. With this in mind, several excellent housing ideas are possible. The Chihuahuas mentioned above sleep in a converted dough tray (without legs) which had a U-shaped opening cut into one side for easy access, and a covered-wagon type of top made of fabric and a bent wire coat hanger. For a larger dog you might remove the doors from a commode or cabinet (keep the hinges attached to the door and store it in an out-of-the-way spot so it can be replaced at a future date if desired), check the interior to be sure it is free from projecting nails, place the dog's mattress and blanket in the base of the commode and he has a protected, draft-free indoor house. The top of the commode can be used as a table to hold a bowl of fruit or flowers.

The family cat might not care for these arrangements. Maybe she would prefer just a large wooden bowl (burl if you can afford it) with a scrunching blanket on which to curl up. Be sure to add a ring of wood or some wooden feet so that the bowl will not rock nor tilt when the cat jumps in and out.

An upholstered footstool placed near your favorite chair might be comfortable for your pet, and keep him off the good furniture.

# Children's Rooms

## INFANTS

THE INFANT IS NOT INTERESTED in his surroundings as far as interior decoration goes. As long as he is warm, fed, and dry, a comfortable cradle is all he will need by way of furniture. Therefore, it is up to Mother to fix up the room as she likes. You may choose traditional pink and blue, or any other color scheme you prefer. Now is a good time to try your hand at quilting, and make a tiny, but washably practical patchwork quilt.

Although a simple cradle will suffice the baby, Mother will require considerably more furniture. Any style furniture can be chosen for the nursery but it would be wise to purchase items with an eye to the future by buying furniture which can be used by the child in later years.

Small-scale chairs are a must; but do not forget to have at least one standard-sized chair, possibly a slat-back rocker or a Boston rocker, for your comfort or for Daddy or Grandmother to pass the time while you fuss over the latest addition.

High chairs are a part of baby's furniture, but they are kept in the kitchen or dining room so are not included here.

Roomy chests of drawers for little clothes are of utmost importance, and a low blanket chest provides storage now and acts as a toy chest later.

## MARBLE TOPS

A marble top commode or chest of drawers is a good place to keep diapers, talcum and baby oil, while the marble top is a convenient height for dressing or changing the baby without having to worry about damaging the finish. A soapy cloth will clean up any accidents and occasional waxings with a paste wax will help protect it. The coolness of the marble will be welcome in summer, and during the winter months a folded bath towel can be placed under the baby.

As the child grows up it will serve other purposes for him. Marble top furniture and children go together like ham and eggs. With the addition of a tall stool (an old bar stool or the kitchen stepping-stool will do) to bring him up to a convenient height, he can have extra play area with the effect similar to the high desks used by architects and draftsmen. The marble top is nearly impervious to finger paints spilled by the budding artist; peanut butter and jelly sandwiches will not harm it, nor will library paste, or even the fishing worms for next Saturday's picnic. It also provides a wonderful place to dump out and assort all manner of treasured "junk" which children are so prone to collect.

## MADE FOR CHILDREN

There was much small-scale furniture made especially for children. These include chairs, rocking chairs, desks, tables and just about the same kinds of furniture you would find in any modern store.

Make sure you buy only sturdy, durable articles as they will receive a lot of hard use.

When finished in the natural wood color, this small furniture is darling against the bright colors that children love. Add a Pennsylvania Dutch chest—or one painted in the same gay, colorful style—and you will have a roomy storage space which the child can use as additional seating area or as a table and play surface.

An old rocking horse will be nice for the toddler.

Consider adding a climbing pole painted in bold stripes à la barber shop. This is accomplished by use of a fireman's pole from a dismantled old firehouse, if you are lucky, or just a smooth metal pipe which is fastened securely at the ceiling and floor and with a round rubber mat around the base. This will fill those rainy days with safe, muscle-building exercise while providing a starting place for imaginative play.

Finish the room with easy-to-care-for linoleum flooring in a stenciled or a spatter pattern, and you will have a room that is as practical as it is attractive.

## CONVERT TO CHILDREN'S USE

Even though there was so much furniture made for children, with some imagination and paint you can extend this amount indefinitely.

The investment in small furniture should be modest as the child is growing rapidly and will need adult size furniture almost before you know it. Therefore, when you buy furniture for Junior, keep an eye open for future use, and buy items that will either grow with the child or can be converted to another use when he outgrows them.

## PAINT

There need be no hesitation in painting antique furniture in gay colors for your child. Many of the new paints are so easy to use and are washable; then later you can remove the paint with no harm done the furniture.

A good many really ugly Victorian and Empire articles will be actually improved by a coat of bright paint. Use semi-gloss paint with a latex base—this can be cleaned up with soap and water, yet dries to a washable finish.

A fussy Gothic Victorian chest of drawers, for example, might be painted a delicate baby pink with white knobs and a thin white line striped around the edges of each drawer. (Striping is easily done with a special kind of brush and is no more difficult than applying nail polish.) Curtains can be made in nylon tulle of the same pastel color chosen for the furniture, resulting in a charming room for a girl. For a boy, the same ungainly furniture might be painted a darker color; maybe a deep, rich blue for all the furniture with curtains and bedspread made of candy striped bed sheets in yellow and white.

If you allow your children to choose their own color schemes and help with the painting, they will not only enjoy their rooms more, but also will have some pride in what they have helped to create, and therefore will take a little better care of it. In some cases, of course, you will have to subtly guide them in order not to have the finished room rival the rainbow.

## NEATNESS

"A place for everything, and everything in its place" is a phrase that obviously came from a well-ordered adult mind. But cheer up, Mom, the antique shops have an answer to that.

Start with the much sneered-at hall tree. Placed strategically near the doorway of Junior's room, it will be the most convenient place for him to toss his jacket when he comes home from school, and a turn toward neatness is begun.

Whatnots have their place in children's rooms. These ungainly open shelves hold all sorts of items, from school books on the bottom shelves to that collection of arrowheads which can be spread out on the topmost shelf. Dainty dolls or rough catchers' mitts; the whatnot is somewhere to keep them until next time they are used. It may not look as attractive as when originally used to hold delicate bric-a-brac, but it will not take up much floor space and will help to keep Junior's treasures from spreading all over the room and across the floor. Whatnots can be painted the color of the walls to make them less conspicuous, or in a bright, contrasting color to be a visual reminder to young children. If two children share the same room, have two whatnots if you can possibly manage the space.

Every child should have a mirror in his room to encourage a neat appearance. There are many styles to choose from.

## SPACE SAVERS

Low blanket chests are easy-to-handle storage bins for toys, and also will provide a combined table, seating and play area. A checkerboard can be painted on the top where it will always be ready for use.

Try placing the bed in the French fashion with the side against the wall. This arrangement will allow more play area in the middle of the room, thus enlarging the room by adding usable space.

A trundle bed is a wonderful space saver if two children share the room, or for the extra guest to a giggly pajama party.

## FOR THE WALLS

A large blackboard from an old school that has been rebuilt or modernized, will give any youngster many happy hours of scribbling and drawing. Mount it on the wall at an appropriate height for the child. By giving him a convenient place on the walls of his own room it will remove the temptation to decorate the walls in the rest of the house. Every lumberyard carries ready-cut picture frame molding which can be purchased by the foot; a wide frame of this will improve the appearance of the blackboard and may be painted in a bright color to contrast with the walls.

While you are at the lumberyard, why not get a piece of beaver board the same size as the blackboard and enough frame for this also, to provide an attractive place for display of drawings, that one hundred per cent spelling test, Christmas cards or pictures of Elvis Presley on the wall opposite from the blackboard. Peg board could be substituted for the beaver board if preferred.

If your house is built with wall board (plaster board or drywall, as it is also called) as so many of the newer houses are, do not hesitate to hang anything heavy. Just make sure you drive the nails into the studs, which should be about 16 inches apart. When you remove the nails in years to come, any little holes remaining in the wall can easily be replastered, and after a coat of paint will completely disappear.

## OLDER CHILDREN

Along with school comes homework which necessitates a desk for performing this highly detested task. Desks range anywhere from pine "schoolmasters" desks to delicate tambour Hepplewhite styles. Many Empire and Victorian desks are available, including the roll tops which hide the scattering of unfinished paperwork. Choosing which style to buy depends a great deal upon the size of the room and the amount of use, not to mention its user.

Growing eyes need good light. Forget about those pretty, small or delicate lamps and put in some non-breakable modern lamps. Keep bright bulbs in the ceiling fixture.

## ALL HIS OWN

A child's room should be colorful, comfortable, and well lighted.

The furniture can be both sturdy enough to withstand the wear and tear imposed by the child's little friends (or fiends in some cases) and yet not heavy nor overpowering for such a small occupant.

Make it a room where the youngster can relax in the wonderful knowledge that it is free of adult tastes. The antiques you buy for your child will depend a great deal upon just how much roughhousing they will have to take. It is better to buy furniture of lesser quality than to constantly nag the children.

# CHAPTER 11

# Bathrooms and Kitchens

## BATHROOMS

THE BATHROOM IS A COMPARATIVELY modern innovation, but that does not mean that it must therefore be a room forgotten by the lover of antiques. By the simple addition of a few accessories, even the smallest bathroom can take on some of the antique charm which flourishes in the other rooms without losing its modern, utilitarian character.

Start by adding a mirror. Any style which pleases you will do; however, the adverse effects of the steam from hot water will be detrimental to any glue, so it is best to avoid veneered examples. Place the mirror opposite the existing mirror in the medicine chest; this will allow you to see the back of your hair for easier setting and for that last minute primping. Dad may spend a little time grumbling about his growing bald spot, but after a while he will get used to seeing it.

Almost any sort of small, hanging cabinet or whatnot can be a useful addition to the bathroom.

A pine spice cabinet does not take up much space while its small drawers will hold all kinds of necessary items to help eliminate clutter in the medicine chest. Its handy drawers can hide such things as bobby pins, hair clips, curlers, small combs, rubber bands for pony tails, nail polish, cotton pads, new razor blades and that orangish lipstick that you only wear with the orange print cotton dress.

A pretty silver or ivory napkin ring can be attached by a thin ribbon to the side or bottom of the spice cabinet. This will provide a handy, wrinkle-free holder for all little daughter's hair ribbons.

If your family prefers tub baths to showers, a hanging salt

box can be placed above the tub for your scented bath salts.

If the size of your bathroom will allow, a shallow cupboard or a small commode will serve for towel storage and at the same time release valuable space in the linen closet. A Victorian washstand takes little space and can be used to hold perfumes, cologne and bath powder as well as be a place for guest towels. A towel rack is still smaller but lacks the table area.

A hall tree would be welcome in the modern bathroom, to hold your robe while you bathe, or, when you have an overnight guest, for that guest towel that has no place. With more limited space, you might look around for a jamb hook which can be attached to the back of the door or the wall, and used for the same purposes.

Brass or other decorative drapery rods can be substituted for the more modern towel racks.

With the color scheme monochromatic (one color, or different shades of one color) and the antiques all finished in their natural wood, the total effect is one of modern efficiency surpassed by antique charm.

# KITCHENS

Today's kitchen is a far cry from the huge open fireplaces with their heavy iron pots suspended by a crane above an open fire. The decorators have said that the modern kitchen is so cold and white that it has the appearance of hospital. This is exaggerating things more than a little, but they have tried to soften the all-white appearance by giving us cabinets of knotty pine or birch in warm tones.

Great-grandmother would have loved the gleaming porcelain surfaces of our everyday appliances. She would have marveled at the ease of using smart white pots and feather-light shiny aluminum pans. She would have thought it a miracle, had she been able to use our modern stoves with their automatic ovens complete with look-through doors, inside lights, and even timing devices to tell us when the pie is done. And, honestly, we feel the same way. We might sigh for the gracious Federal days of

Washington and Jefferson, but we would not give up our modern conveniences for anything.

There is nothing incongruous about antiques in the kitchen. Many of the utensils we use are the same as have been used by women as long as they have been cooking for their men. The changes have been primarily in material, today's lighter metals being much easier to handle and care for than those of the past.

Despite improvements, many items have come down to us in exactly the same shape as used more than a century ago. Antique cooking spoons, forks, and ladles can be used today, needing only to be scrubbed thoroughly and scalded to be ready for making dinner.

Two-tined eating forks are handy to use as cooking forks when the smaller size is called for, thus saving your good silver. Iron forks may need sharpening, which can be easily done without diminishing their value.

Woodenware consists of many articles from slightly warped bowls and buckets through elegant burl bowls and down to simple paddles. The wooden paddle, such as the pudding paddle, is a cross between a spoon and a stick. The paddle's shape is similar in outline to a spoon, differing mainly in that it does not have a bowl on the end. This is a great boon to the cook when stirring batter, for the paddle can be scraped clean against the side of the pan without that annoying bit of batter remaining in the indentation of the spoon's bowl which necessitates either vigorous hitting against the side of the pan or scraping with the finger. Once these quaint wooden items are used, you will realize that they are equal to, and in many instances superior to, their modern counterparts. The author would not be without them in her kitchen.

"Water on wood" is decried in many circles. Do not let wooden articles soak in water, but on the other hand there is no reason not to apply soap and hot water liberally. Wood will shrink and even warp slightly, but this is a small price to pay for sanitation with objects that come into contact with our food—after all, they are antiques, and therefore cannot be expected to be in mint condition. An occasional light oiling with any good salad oil will be beneficial to counteract the drying effect of repeated washings. Just pour a little salad oil on a soft cloth and polish the wood, let stand a few minutes, then wipe off any excess. The author was doing just this to her antique wooden utensils one Saturday afternoon when friend Husband walked in inquiring, "What're you doing, dear?" "Just oiling my woodenware," came the reply to which patient Husband stared in horror. It seems that he had been oiling some garden tools with crude oil just the evening before and thought . . . well you can take it from there.

Since so many kitchens have eating space, you might consider a hutch table (also called a chair table or a settle table). This handy kind of table will add extra feet of usable space to your kitchen. The hutch table is made with a seat in the base and a top which tilts, becoming the back for the chair. It requires very little space when the top is up and some even have a drawer in the base which can be used to store table linens, thus giving it a three-way use. In modern furniture this would be called functional; in antiques, just good sense.

If the room size permits, there are many attractive corner cupboards, Welsh dressers and cupboards of all sizes to give you storage space and show off your pretty china or that collection of colored glass or pewter.

Pierced tin pie-cupboards are generally shallow and take up little room.

Marble-top commodes and dry sinks by the door as noted in Chapter 3 can be convenient.

Hanging cupboards are extremely handy. They are generally heavy, but can be attached to the wall securely by means of large picture hooks on the top and L-shaped brackets on the bottom.

Additional counter top space can be had in even the smallest kitchen by a little nagging of friend Husband. The simple addition is made by using a broken-off drop leaf from a discarded table or a small table top which is minus its legs, or even a fancy grained breadboard of ample dimensions. By attaching this to the kitchen wall with hinges and adding a small wooden bracket beneath, it can become an extra table, taking up only a few inches when not needed by folding down against the wall similarly to the drop leaf on a butterfly or gate-leg table. It is preferable not to put any finish on the wood, so that it can be used for foodstuffs and washed as often as necessary. A little salad oil rubbed in occasionally will keep the wood in good condition and will bring out the beauty of the grain.

Spice cabinets belong in the kitchen, but have you thought of using them for holding such items as string, rubber bands, tacks, safety pins, paper clips, extra collar stays where they will be handy when you iron, trading stamps, and all those little articles which are so necessary yet seldom handy when needed?

The black color of old iron compliments light or pastel colors —another reason that it has become so very popular in the kitchen. Such utensils as forks, both eating and cooking varieties, trivets, muffin tins, apple corers, chopping knives, and bootjacks all belong in the kitchen anyway. A cast iron pot or kettle can be used to hold a large potted plant or to keep paper bags handy.

Black iron muffin tins in their myriad of shapes are very decorative. Useful, too, they are perfect for baking small rolls, individual pastries, fancily shaped tarts, and petits fours which bake as easily as cookies (just pour your cake batter in to half-full, bake in hot oven and they will be done in about twelve minutes; cool, pour thin, tinted frosting over them and you are ready for the bridge club meeting). When you want to make a lot of baked potatoes at one time, stand them in one of the muffin tins for easier handling; it is quicker and there is less chance of getting burned.

Towel-dry iron articles thoroughly so they will not rust. If they should get a little rusty, kerosene and steel wool will remedy the condition.

Trivets are especially attractive surrounding a stove where they are most needed. Also various ladles, forks, and spoons hung in a grouping ready for use can decorate the wall back of the stove.

There is always enough room for hanging kitchen utensils where they can be decorative as well as useful. A symmetrical arrangement is usually the most attractive.

Unusual or colorful plates and platters can be hung on special plate racks so that they resemble pictures.

Sugar shakers in pretty painted china, silver, or pewter to suit your taste, can be used for sugar-cinnamon mixture on the breakfast table or for holding your cooking salt next to the stove. Colored sugars can be sprinkled on cookies more evenly with one of these dainty articles, as can flour for rolling out pastry dough. They can also be used for grated cheese at the table.

Master salts are as numerous as they are varied in design. They were made in quantity in any size, shape or pattern you could want. In our home we use these tiny containers for many items: heading the list is salad dressing—the boss uses it while his chief-cook-and-bottle-washer does not—it is simple to prepare one serving of mayonnaise or Russian dressing in a salt dish, using a tiny salt spoon for serving. Master salts can also be used for individual servings of relishes, ketchup, mustard, mint, apple sauce, cranberry sauce, tartar sauce, or melted butter. Use the master salt dishes; the individual salts are too small for a sufficient serving.

A small slate (blackboard) of the kind used by school children, hung near the kitchen door along with a piece of chalk suspended by some string from the same nail, is a good place to keep your shopping list. It can also be a constant reminder for that easily forgotten chore or special date, since it is difficult to avoid seeing it every time you enter or leave through the back door. (The printed memo of "fix doorbell" is a challenge which Husband soon answers without another word from you, just so he can erase the accusing words staring at him.)

While you are near the back door with that hammer and nail, make a place for your bootjack; it will save you from ruining your manicure struggling with galoshes in the winter.

Pewter and silver porringers are as lovely to look at as they are to use, but alas, not always easy to find. Here is another of those times when reproductions are useful. There are several old silver companies that have been making the same style porringers for more than a hundred years, as well as other firms which make excellent copies in numerous sizes. The larger porringers adapt themselves readily to cereal, fruit and milk, soup, or candy dishes. The little porringers can be used for a bouillon-cup sized serving of soup; this is just enough to start the meal without being overfilling. (One can of condensed soup used this way will make four or five attractive portions.)

The kitchen is such a nice sunny place for plants that you might want to complete your kitchen with some planters converted from salt boxes, glass lamps, bird cages, or anything else which amuses you.

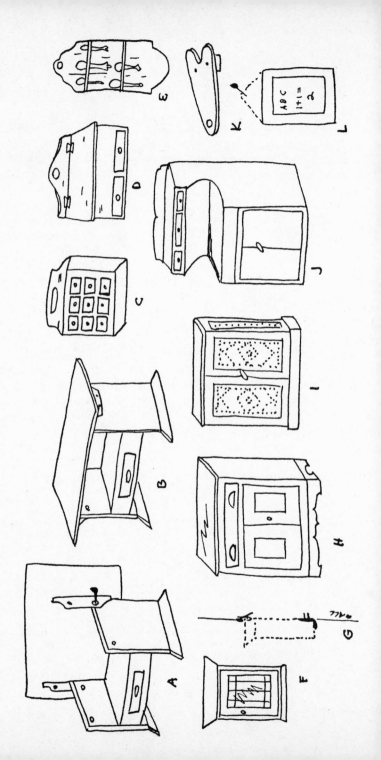

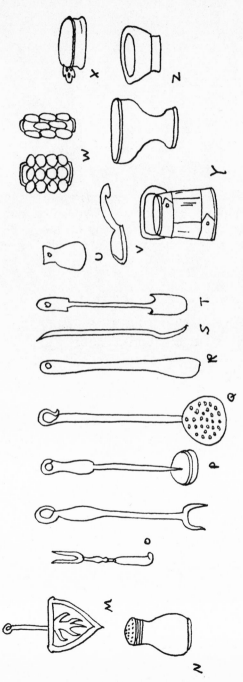

## KITCHENS

A hutch table, up, *B* hutch table, down, *C*, *D* spice chests, *E* spoon rack, *F* hanging cupboard, *G* shows how to attach a heavy article to wall with large picture hooks and *L* brackets, *H* marble-top commode, *I* pierced tin pie cupboard, *J* dry sink, *K* bootjack, *L* slate, *M* trivet, *N* sugar shaker, *O* iron forks, *P* ladle, *Q* skimmer, *R* wooden paddle, *S* side view of wooden spoon, *T* pudding paddle, *U* dough paddle, *V* butter paddle, *W* iron muffin "tins," *X* porringer, *Y* wooden bucket, *Z* master salts.

# Whether to Modernize Antiques

## CONVERT TO ANOTHER USE

WHETHER TO MODERNIZE or not often depends upon what is meant by the use of the word "modernize." If by that you mean to make the item more usable for modern living by using it for another purpose than the one for which it was made—by all means do it.

## DON'T MUTILATE

But, on the other hand, if what is meant by the word modernized is to convert it by cutting the article down, or by any other major change—*no!*

Don't sand!

Don't saw!

Don't separate or substitute parts!

By doing any of these things you mutilate your antique and thereby lose any value it has as an antique. It then becomes merely an oddity. Any repair or restoration, no matter how necessary, decreases the value of an antique. To remake it into another article entirely will result in a complete loss of value as an antique.

So, let this rule be foremost in your mind: Do Not Mutilate.

## COFFEE TABLES

Coffee tables, or cocktail tables if you prefer, are a recent development. You can find numerous small tables from tea tables to Pembroke tables which served our ancestors in the same general capacity; but not the low tables to set in front of the sofa as we use them today.

The fireplace was at one time the heart of the home. This one is from the Buffalo Historical Society.

T.V. and telephones are a part of our lives today and can be harmonious with antiques. The drop-leaves of this curly maple table are of one wide plank.

A vast improvement over cooking in an open fireplace, the modern kitchen is at ease with useful antiques. A hutch table saves valuable space and Windsor chairs are always comfortable.

Even a tiny bathroom can benefit by the addition of a few antique items. Hall tree, mirror and marble-top commode are shown here.

A pleasant corner for sewing or reading: Victorian vintage rocker, and primitive lift-top blanket chest with cotter-pin hinges and leather strap for closing. The knitting bowl is a reproduction.

This bird's-eye maple secretary makes a fine place for displaying a collection or a hobby.

Some people use such unlikely articles as cobblers' benches and wagon seats for coffee tables. Even large blacksmith's bellows are dismantled and made into coffee tables by the addition of turned legs. These may be amusing in an informal game room, but hardly seem suitable for your living room.

Tables of all shapes have been converted by having their legs cut down to coffee table height; marble-top Victorian tables being the most fashionable for this practice.

It is difficult to say, "No, never cut down an antique," in this particular instance, because of the widespread use of the coffee table and the lack of an antique counterpart. This piece of furniture serves as a receptacle for ash trays, cigarettes, flower bowl, magazines, the daily newspaper, and is so extremely convenient that it would be hard to do without it.

Therefore it is up to you to decide for yourself whether to cut down an antique and thus decrease its value, or to have made a coffee table that will blend in with your other antique furnishings. If you do decide to convert an antique table, do not mutilate a valuable one, rather use a later or a poorer specimen.

## PAINTING

There need be no hesitation to paint and decorate antique furniture. Paint can be removed without injuring the surface of the wood by using commercial paint remover and steel wool.

Paint at one time was made with Venetian red (at a cost of two cents a pound) or brick dust (which could be had for the scraping) mixed with skimmed milk. This proved to be a cheap, strong paint which lasted a remarkably long time. In refinishing antique furniture this is extremely difficult to remove, requiring many hours and much labor.

Today's superior paints are easy to use. Some of the newer paints are of the wonderful water-thinned type such as the latex based. Fast drying and odorless, they can be cleaned up with soap and water. Spills and brushes can be easily washed clean; no longer do you have to put up with smelly turpentine and messy brushes. These paints are easy to use, go on smoothly and dry

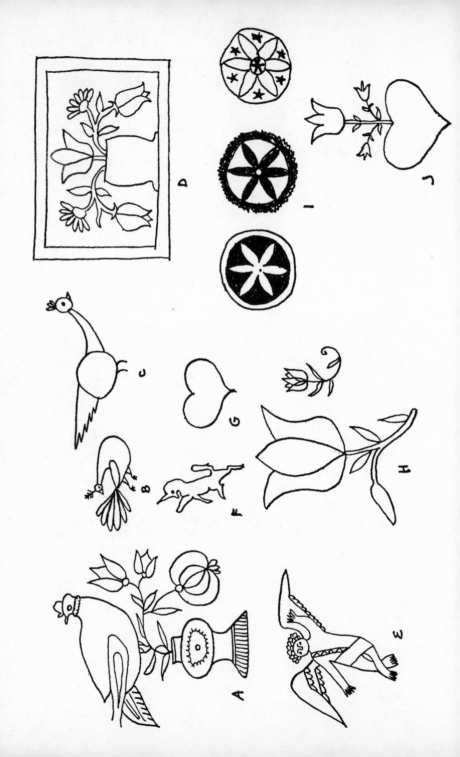

## DESIGNS

*A, B, C* Pennsylvania Dutch birds, *D* panel from decorated chest, *E* angel, *F* unicorn, *G* heart, *H* tulips, *I* hex signs painted on barns, *J* heart-and-tulip pattern (all of these are typical of Pennsylvania Dutch), *K* stencil of the type used circa 1820 by Hitchcock and others for furniture, *L, M* two simple designs easy to copy, *N, O* eagles.

quickly to a fine, washable finish. Semi-gloss is the best finish for furniture.

These newer paints are especially appreciated by all of you week-end do-it-yourselfers who often get as much paint on yourself as on the object you intended to decorate. With modern paints it is even easier to just go ahead and do it yourself than to keep after Husband to do it for you. A few newspapers on the floor, an hour's time, then wash your hands and brush in soapy water. There are several companies that produce this latex-base kind of paint. A simple perusal of the instructions as printed upon the back of the can of paint will give you the necessary information.

Simple designs look good on some furniture. Pennsylvania Dutch motifs are appealing to all ages, so if you feel artistic you might copy these amusing decorations. The simpler stencils of the kind used by Hitchcock are also appropriate.

Painted furniture has been in vogue over many years and through many different styles and periods. Lacquered furniture is reported to have been imported to England as early as 1675.

The fact that some articles are composed of several different kinds of wood is mute testimony to the fact that they were painted from the very beginning.

All kinds of furniture were decorated; from impressive high-boys and secretary-bookcases, chests and tables of many sorts, through gay, colorful designs executed by the Pennsylvania Dutch people, down to the fancy chairs mass-produced by Hitchcock and his contemporaries.

The amount and kind of decoration you decide upon for the article you want to paint will be determined by your artistic ability. Tauton chests have an easy-to-copy style of line drawings in white on a dark background with tiny daubs of one color; Hitchcock-type chairs are done with gold or bronze powders in stenciled motifs; Hepplewhite and Sheraton used delicate paintings to orna-ment some of their furniture. The Pennsylvania Dutch designs, so quaint and symbolic, are charming: fat hearts, tulips, peacocks, hex signs of stars within circles, are characteristic. Eagles have been popular since Federal days (after 1776).

A plain solid color with just a thin line of another color

striped around the edge of the drawers and along the edge of the table top requires only a fifteen-cent striping brush and is as easy as applying nail polish.

## ELECTRIFYING

There are simple converters available which screw on to oil lamps in place of the original burner, and immediately turn them into electric lamps. These are made in several popular sizes and are inexpensive.

Gone-With-the-Wind lamps require a more elaborate wiring and should be electrified by an expert.

Besides old lamps there are many other items and *objets d'art* which can be successfully made into attractive lamps. Any nicely shaped vase, urn, or bowl which will look good with the other furniture of the room for which it is intended will be appropriate. These, too, should be given to a professional to electrify, for the amateur can easily crack or break them by not having the proper tools nor the experience necessary. It is cheaper to pay for having a lovely vase converted into a lamp than to risk breaking it, thereby losing your complete investment.

Amusing shapes in copper and brass are often made into lamps, including such unlikely shapes as teapots, completed with pierced colanders for shades.

Turned wood of a pleasing shape, and carved wood from a broken pedestal table or a broken four-poster bed, will sometimes make a pretty lamp base; needing only to have a hole drilled down through the middle plus the addition of electric parts.

Nearly anything can be, and is being, converted into lamps. The only limitation is your own imagination.

Be sure to avoid using anything which will prove top-heavy or easily tipped over when converted. If you must have that particular item made into a lamp be sure to have the base weighted.

After choosing your lamp base and having it electrified, comes the problem of choosing the shade. Frequently the shade will cost more than the lamp itself. One couple found this out recently when the wife bought a vase with a hole already drilled in the bottom for the bargain price of only fifty cents. "Just the thing for the guest room," she told her husband, "and it will hardly cost anything." The electric parts came to less than two dollars but despite much searching the least expensive shade found which would look good with the base cost over eight dollars. "But the base *was* such a bargain." (And what woman can pass up a bargain?)

Although it may seem awkward at the time, it is best to take the lamp base with you when you go shopping for a shade. Measurements may be accurate, but cannot give you the completed appearance; only by actually trying the shades on your lamp will you be able to see just how it will look in your house.

# Novel and Modern Uses
# for Antiques

A LARGE NUMBER of antique articles have little or no practical use today other than that of decorative value.

Often these same articles can be used for other purposes than those for which they were originally designed, without any alterations or disfiguring changes. Thus the item is kept intact, retaining its charm as an antique, yet serving a useful household purpose.

It is the vogue today to use anything possible for a planter, and what cannot serve to hold plants is then converted into a lamp base. Many unlikely articles have been used with ridiculous results.

Other than these common uses and mis-uses, there are unlimited ways to make the pretty little articles you collect work for you.

Here then, are a few ideas:

## BIRD CAGE

Makes an unusual planter. A clay pot with several house plants—one or two of which should be trailing vines, such as philodendron—will be sufficient. Place on a stand or hang on a bracket for a delightful sight in the breakfast room. If you have a patio you might decide to hang a planted bird cage outside during the summer months.

A little wooden or pottery bird in fancy (or even fantastic) colors will be a cheerful touch.

## BUTTER CHURN

Its size makes a butter churn ideal as a clothes hamper for a small bathroom. Make sure the inside is smooth, and sand, if necessary, to protect clothing.

Can be used as an umbrella stand, or made into the base for a standing lamp.

## BUTTONHOOKS

Every home should have at least one long-handled button hook. You never know when some small item will fall into an inaccessible spot. Often a buttonhook will save you the effort of moving a large piece of furniture in order to reach something which is maddeningly just out of reach.

Also useful for threading a wire or piece of string through a narrow opening, and removing hair caught in the sink drain. Keep the hook either in your sewing basket or in your Husband's tool case.

## WOODEN BUCKET

A small wooden bucket makes a good wastebasket. Or in the kitchen one can be used as a holder for those necessary evils— paper bags.

## CANDLEMOLD

Glass vials purchased at your drugstore to fit into the candle-mold will convert it into a charming flower holder. The individual vials can be filled with flowers and leaves, or cuttings of such greens as ivy or wandering Jew which will root and grow in water.

## CARD TABLE

So often used as a side table, it seldom is used for its original purpose for playing cards, chess or checkers.

## CHAMBER POT

A convenient size to hold a large potted plant. Also can be used for a wastebasket next to a bedroom dressing table.

Chamber pots can be sterilized and used for soup tureens or punch bowls.

## COLANDER

Made of tin, copper, or brass, it can be used for a ceiling-fixture shade in an informal room. If you must have a kettle or a pot for a lamp base, here is a novel lamp shade for it.

## COOKIE JAR

Any large glass jar with a cover can be used for a cookie jar. Large apothecary jars are often used this way, as are old candy bottles from grocery stores. Use your nail polish and an orange stick to paint small polka dots evenly around the jar for a gay, yet simple decoration; or, if you are artistic, use the little brush to paint sprigs of flowers with a wavy line top and bottom. This makes a washable decoration that can be changed or removed whenever you tire of it.

## CRADLE

If your child is a girl then the cradle can become a doll's bed after she has outgrown it.

Some use cradles to hold magazines or firewood by the fireplace.

## CRANBERRY SCOOP

Makes a nice fruit bowl for a center arrangement at the table. Can be hung on the wall to hold a potted plant.

## STONEWARE CROCK

A good place to store small articles since it is waterproof and can be set upon the basement floor or in a damp garage.

In the kitchen, a stoneware crock can hold the paper bag containing garbage until you can take it outside.

Filled with ice cubes and cold water, it can keep many soft drink bottles cold for your outdoor barbecues.

## CUP PLATES

Can be used as spoon rests when you are cooking, or on the table for resting the end of the carving knife. They are the right size to use as coasters for small juice glasses, and for syrup pitchers or ketchup at the table.

## DECOYS

Many use them for mantel decorations. If the decoys are heavy enough, they can also be used for book ends.

Place them in the garden, nestled amid a clump of flowers, or sitting nonchalantly in a vegetable garden surrounded by tomatoes and carrots.

## DOUGH TRAY

When used as an end table next to the sofa, it can become the storage place for extra bedding for an overnight guest.

As a lamp table, the storage area inside the dough tray can become a good place to keep those extra light bulbs, ash trays, and the candy dish when not in use.

## DRY SINK

For a garden center near the kitchen door and for foyer or mud room to hold necessities for inclement weather as noted in chapter 3. Can be filled with potted plants surrounded with sphagnum moss for a pretty dining room addition.

## FLOWER CONTAINER

Bowls and vases are not the only flower containers. Even a wooden mortar (with or without pestle) can be used if kitchen aluminum foil is used to line it and then a small glass or jar is set securely into it. Aluminum foil, floral arranger's clay, empty jelly glasses and imagination can turn almost anything into a vase. A few extra leaves will hide the mechanics of your arrangement.

Wooden articles make lovely seasonal containers for autumn arrangements; iron items can be used without worry of rust; porous articles can be utilized; and leaking vases used again by this method.

## FOOT WARMER

Filled with a few charcoal briquettes, it will generate enough heat to keep rolls (on a sheet of aluminum foil) warm while you barbecue the hot dogs and hamburgers. Also helps keep second helpings warm without burning.

## HAND-WROUGHT NAILS

When they can be obtained, hand-wrought nails are decorative enough to use for hanging pictures and other items. The nail itself harmonizes with primitive articles and enhances their charm.

## INKWELLS

Use as floral containers for small, delicate flowers. Will be appropriate for a desk.

## IRONS

Heavy sadirons make excellent door stoppers. The smaller flatirons are often painted and used in pairs as book ends.

## JAMB HOOKS

Brass jamb hooks, well polished and covered with colorless nail polish to keep them from tarnishing, can be affixed to the back of the door or the wall in the bathroom or a closet as a clothes hook. In the kitchen they will hold towels or your apron. Put one on the wall next to your sewing machine, or on the side of the machine itself—it will be invaluable.

## KEROSENE LAMPS

Besides using them as they are for outdoor lighting in the summer and for emergency lightning in the case of a power failure, they can be used several other ways.

Miniature lamps, five or six inches tall, can be kept burning on the coffee table or buffet during a party to act as handy cigarette lighters; just turn up the wick for easy lighting and turn back down to low again. They are as practical as they are quaint.

Wall brackets with glass lamps make attractive planters for ivy or other trailing plants, and are particularly cheerful in kitchen and dining rooms. Any kind of kerosene lamp can be used as a planter.

## KETTLES

A small kettle makes a good watering can for house plants. Brass or copper kettles are often made into lamp bases.

## KNIFE BOX

An excellent container for garden tools because of the ease in carrying. Trowel, pruning shears, labels, seeds, and gardening gloves can be toted in one hand. This saves many steps. Convenient for carrying cut flowers in one side while the other holds the dead leaves and faded flowers you prune off, thus you can do in one trip what would otherwise require two.

Cleaned up and waxed, a knife box can be used as a quaint fruit bowl.

Kept near the washer, it can hold those loose buttons and be handy to receive the holey socks and other mending when you sort your clean laundry.

## OLD KNIVES AND TWO-TINED FORKS

Difficult to eat with, they still can be useful in other ways: For fruit and cheese knives, and the two-tined forks can be used as serving utensils for cold cuts, etc.

In cooking, the obsolete dinner forks can be often used where a larger cooking fork is not needed, thus saving wear and tear on your good silver.

## LOTION BOTTLES

Rescued from an old barbershop, these are ideal for bud vases. They can hold a single flower to provide a touch of elegance to your dinner table, or to put on that small lamp table.

## MOUSTACHE CUPS

Clear soups such as tomato or bouillon can be drunk from a moustache cup, with the little "shelf" for the moustache being a dry spot to hold small croutons. Handy, if you wish to watch television or read the newspaper while eating. Hot chocolate or cocoa, with the shelf holding cookies, is a good after-school treat on cold days.

Can be used to pour batter for pancakes. Also, they make good syrup or milk pitchers for young children because there is less chance of them spilling the contents.

## MUFFIN TINS

Numerous shapes made of cast iron can be used for making easy petits fours, rolls, individual pastries, tarts, or holding baked potatoes when you are baking a large amount. (It is easy to put in a few extra potatoes to mash, then return to shells, and store in the refrigerator for twice-baked potatoes the next day.)

A handy item for the basement workshop. Husband can separate small parts when he does repairs for you, keeping them safe and sorted in a muffin tin; no more searching for that lost part which always rolls under the water heater.

## NAPKIN RINGS

Napkin rings are just the right size to hide a small needlepoint holder for flowers in low bowl arrangements. Silver rings are especially lovely with silver bowls filled with roses on the dinner table. Noted as holders for hair ribbons in chapter 11.

## OPEN GREASE LAMPS

Good for holding matches over a fireplace.

## PICTURE FRAMES

Can become trays with the addition of a piece of plywood across the bottom and some paint.

## PITCHERS

Use to water house plants, or to hold a bouquet of flowers. Used on the table, they can hold anything from gravy to syrup.

## PLANTERS

Almost anything and everything can be made into a planter. Just look around; consider the color and texture of the proposed container in relation to the type of plant or flower you are going to use. Keep silver, glass, satin glass, alabaster, and porcelain for the more delicate flowers, such as roses, lilacs and violets; wooden, iron, and coarse pottery are more suited to marigolds, zinnias and daisies. Philodendron and ivy look good in almost any sort of planter, but Sansevieria (mother-in-law's tongue) looks better in heavy or coarse pottery.

## PORRINGER

Usually used for cereal (hot or dry), soup, and puddings. Also they can be used for candy dishes or ash trays.

The handles makes them easy to carry around; records tell of how the Pilgrims stood before the fireplace on cold mornings eating from their porringers. You can use them the same way by filling up a porringer full of nourishing cereal or soup for your youngster who can be getting his vitamins while watching television.

## POTS AND CAULDRONS

Iron, brass or copper, they are used for wastebaskets or nice-looking jardinieres for holding plants potted in clay pots. Damaged brass and copper pots can be used for outdoor planters with the leaky bottoms providing the necessary drainage. Coat with lacquer to avoid constant polishing.

## SALT BOXES

Pine salt boxes can be hung on the wall to hold a potted plant. They can also be used to hold bath salts above the tub or soap flakes above the washing machine.

## SALT DISHES

There are endless uses for the darling little containers known as "master salts" and made of glass, silver, pewter or wood. They can be used for individual servings at the table as noted in chapter 11.

Also they make dainty flower bowls for miniature roses or

other small posies. A tiny needlepoint frog can be set in the bottom or vermiculate or fine gravel can be used to hold the flowers. These are an ideal size for just a few little flowers and they are small enough to be placed upon a window sill above the kitchen sink for a cheerful sight above the dish pan. Their size enables you to have a miniature bouquet on any table, desk or shelf.

## SALT SPOONS

Good for filling or removing contents from small bottles. Can be used for adding face powder to your compact. When using salts for individual servings of food stuffs, these little spoons become serving spoons.

## SHAVING MUGS

Use as soup bowls for informal luncheons. As children find these particularly amusing, they can be used to encourage lagging appetites.

Also can be used for hearty portions of coffee or hot chocolate on a cold day.

## SNUFF BOXES

Use to hold pins: straight or safety. A pretty way to keep pins handy in bedroom, kitchen or laundry.

Can hold postage stamps on the desk.

Snuff boxes can hold little pills on the night stand or even on the dining table when a member of the family is ill or needs extra vitamins.

## SPICE CABINETS

Covered at length in chapter 11. Can also be used to house sewing articles when hung just above sewing machine.

## LARGE STATUES AND BUSTS

If made of iron or pottery they make delightful focal spots in a small garden. Grow short plants such as pansies, alyssum or petunias around the bases and a taller bush behind for a green background. Iron will need a coat or two of exterior paint so that it will not rust.

## STICKPINS

Can be easily made into charms for a bracelet, tie tacks for your Husband, or scatter pins for yourself. An especially pretty stickpin could be mounted on to a ring for a very little girl. A group of stickpins can be arranged into a bouquet and affixed to a brooch to make an attractive lapel pin. Used as they are, they can be novel ornaments on a hat.

## SUGAR SHAKERS

Can be used for sugar and cinnamon mixture for the table or for grated cheese.

They make good salt shakers for cooking. Household chores are so much more pleasant with beautiful tools. Used for flour, a sugar shaker can make flouring meat, thickening gravy or rolling out pastry dough much easier.

Sugar shakers can be used to display thin-stemmed dried flowers or to house a collection of long-stemmed hat pins. Ideal for powdered sugar for cookies and cakes.

## TOWEL RACKS

Useful when ironing, mending or sewing to hold the garments and keep them from wrinkling.

## WOOD BIN

Useful as a clothes hamper, it probably will need sanding on the inside. Can be used as a toy bin also.

# NEW WAYS

*A* knife box, *B* iron cauldron, *C* cast-iron wall bracket and glass lamp, *D* miniature kerosene lamp, *E, F* jamb hooks, *G* candle mold, *H* foot warmer, *I* wooden mug, *J, K* salts, *L* slate, *M* button hook, *N* chamber pot, *O* sadiron, *P* portable desk, *Q* marble-top commode, *R* spice chest, *S* forks, *T* hand-wrought nail, *U* shaving mug, *V* sugar shaker, *W* towel rack, *X* snuff box, *Y* butter churn, *Z* decoy.

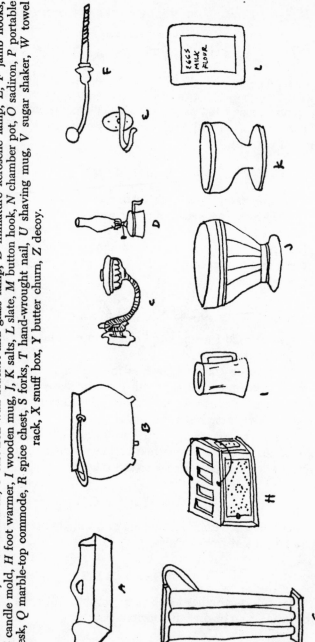

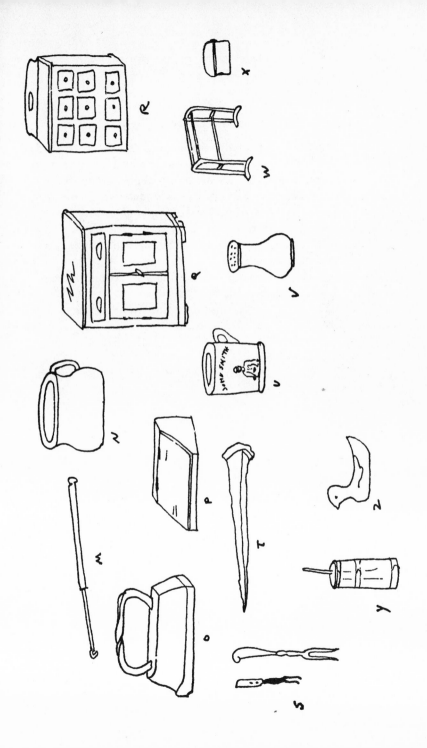

## WRITING BOXES
## (PORTABLE DESKS)

Their portability makes them a natural for those few odd moments when you are doing something which requires your presence intermittently: When dinner is almost ready and the table is set, you often have ten or fifteen minutes while the roast reheats and the potatoes get done; baking cookies requires you to be ready when the oven timer signals, yet in these few minutes you can sit down and get that letter written to Aunt Minnie if the portable desk is kept nearby.

A writing box can be used for a sewing box. Its compartments are divided for such a purpose very well.

It can also be used for a trinket container, holding all sorts of odd items which have no other home.


These are just a few ideas; use your own imagination and you will find many more.